D0963448

AFTER 9/11

AFTER 9/11

AMERICA'S WAR ON TERROR (2001–)

**Sid Jacobson
and
Ernie Colón**

A NOVEL GRAPHIC from HILL AND WANG

A division of FARRAR, STRAUS AND GIROUX NEW YORK

Hill and Wang
A division of Farrar, Straus and Giroux
18 West 18th Street, New York 10011

Distributed in Canada by Douglas & McIntyre Ltd.
Printed in the United States of America
Published simultaneously in hardcover and paperback
First edition, 2008

Library of Congress Cataloging-in-Publication Data
Jacobson, Sidney.
    After 9/11 : America's war on terror (2001–) / Sid Jacobson and Ernie
Colón.
        p. cm.
    "A novel graphic."
    ISBN-13: 978-0-8090-2357-8 (hardcover : alk. paper)
    ISBN-10: 0-8090-2357-1 (hardcover : alk. paper)
    1. War on Terrorism, 2001– —Pictorial works. 2. Terrorism—Government
policy—United States—Pictorial works. 3. United States—Politics and
government—2001– —Pictorial works. 4. Afghan War, 2001– —Pictorial works.
5. Iraq War, 2003– —Pictorial works. I. Colón, Ernie. II. Title. III. Title: After
September 11th.

HV6432.J37 2008
973.931—dc22   2008013298

Paperback ISBN-13: 978-0-8090-2370-7
Paperback ISBN-10: 0-8090-2370-9

www.fsgbooks.com

10 9 8 7 6 5 4 3 2 1

This book draws upon the work of print, sound, and visual media across the globe.
The authors were especially inspired by *The New York Times*, the *Los Angeles
Times*, *The Washington Post*, *Time*, *Newsweek*, and *The New Yorker*, as well as the
polling services of CBS, ABC, and Gallup.

CONTENTS

Prologue 3

Chapter 1: America Responds 5

Chapter 2: War in Afghanistan 11

Chapter 3: Victory? 20

Chapter 4: The Selling of a War 32

Chapter 5: The Making of a War 45

Chapter 6: Insurgency or Civil War? 65

Chapter 7: The Surge 129

Epilogue 149

AFTER 9/11

PROLOGUE

"DO YOU THINK THE U.S. OR UN FORCES SHOULD HAVE MOVED INTO BAGHDAD?"

NO.

"WHY NOT?"

BECAUSE IF WE'D GONE INTO BAGHDAD, WE WOULD HAVE BEEN ALONE. THERE WOULDN'T HAVE BEEN ANYBODY ELSE WITH US. THERE WOULD HAVE BEEN A U.S. OCCUPATION OF IRAQ. NONE OF THE ARAB FORCES THAT WERE WILLING TO FIGHT WITH US IN KUWAIT WERE WILLING TO INVADE IRAQ.

ONCE YOU GOT INTO IRAQ AND TOOK IT OVER, TOOK DOWN SADDAM HUSSEIN'S GOVERNMENT, THEN WHAT ARE YOU GOING TO PUT IN ITS PLACE?

THAT'S A VERY VOLATILE PART OF THE WORLD, AND IF YOU TAKE DOWN THE CENTRAL GOVERNMENT OF IRAQ, YOU COULD VERY EASILY END UP SEEING PIECES OF IRAQ FLY OFF.

PART OF IT, THE SYRIANS WOULD LIKE TO HAVE THE WEST. PART OF IT--EASTERN IRAQ--THE IRANIANS WOULD LIKE TO CLAIM. THEY FOUGHT OVER IT FOR EIGHT YEARS. IN THE NORTH YOU'VE GOT THE KURDS, AND IF THE KURDS SPIN LOOSE AND JOIN WITH THE KURDS IN TURKEY, THEN YOU THREATEN THE TERRITORIAL INTEGRITY OF TURKEY.

IT'S A QUAGMIRE IF YOU GO THAT FAR AND TRY TO TAKE OVER IRAQ.

THE OTHER THING WAS CASUALTIES. EVERYONE WAS IMPRESSED WITH THE FACT THAT WE WERE ABLE TO DO OUR JOB WITH AS FEW CASUALTIES AS WE HAD. BUT FOR THE 146 AMERICANS KILLED IN ACTION AND FOR THEIR FAMILIES, IT WASN'T A CHEAP WAR. AND THE QUESTION FOR THE PRESIDENT IN TERMS OF WHETHER OR NOT WE WENT ON TO BAGHDAD AND TOOK ADDITIONAL CASUALTIES IN AN EFFORT TO GET SADDAM HUSSEIN WAS, HOW MANY ADDITIONAL DEAD AMERICANS IS SADDAM WORTH? AND OUR JUDGMENT WAS NOT VERY MANY, AND I THINK WE GOT IT RIGHT.

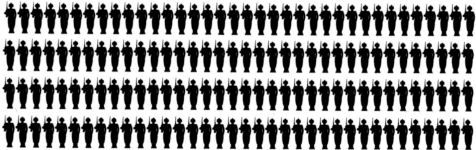

...WHEN TWO HIJACKED JETLINERS TARGETED AND DESTROYED THE WORLD TRADE CENTER TOWERS IN NEW YORK CITY...WHILE A THIRD HIJACKED JETLINER TARGETED AND HIT THE PENTAGON IN ARLINGTON, VIRGINIA...

...AND A FOURTH HIJACKED PLANE, PREVENTED FROM HITTING ANOTHER WASHINGTON, D.C., AREA TARGET BY ITS HEROIC PASSENGERS, CRASHED ONTO A FIELD IN SHANKSVILLE, PENNSYLVANIA.

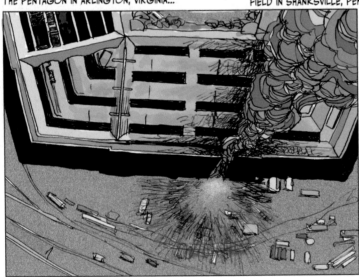

ALL THOSE ABOARD THE FOUR AIRPLANES WERE KILLED THAT DAY, AS WELL AS THOUSANDS INSIDE THE TARGETED BUILDINGS. TWO OF THE FOUR FLIGHTS ORIGINATED AT BOSTON'S LOGAN AIRPORT, ONE AT NEWARK'S LIBERTY AIRPORT, AND A FOURTH AT WASHINGTON'S DULLES AIRPORT. ALL WERE SLATED TO FLY TO CALIFORNIA AND CARRIED FULL TANKS OF FUEL.

THAT NIGHT, PRESIDENT BUSH, SPEAKING FROM THE OVAL OFFICE, PROMISED TO RETALIATE AGAINST THE PARTIES RESPONSIBLE FOR THESE ATTACKS AND SAID THAT HE WOULD...

...MAKE NO DISTINCTION BETWEEN THE TERRORISTS WHO COMMITTED THESE ACTS AND THOSE WHO HARBOR THEM.

OUR COUNTRY IS STRONG. TERRORIST ACTS CAN SHAKE THE FOUNDATION OF OUR HIGHEST BUILDINGS, BUT THEY CANNOT SHAKE THE FOUNDATION OF AMERICA.

ONLY HOURS AFTER THE ATTACKS, AMERICAN COUNTERTERRORISM EXPERTS ANNOUNCED THAT ELECTRONIC EAVESDROPPING INTERCEPTS INDICATED THAT OSAMA BIN LADEN, A WEALTHY ISLAMIC MILITANT, AND HIS TERRORIST GROUP, AL QAEDA, ENCAMPED IN AND PROTECTED BY AFGHANISTAN, WERE THE RESPONSIBLE PARTIES.

*MULLAH MOHAMMED OMAR, NOW IN HIDING, WAS THE LEADER OF THE TALIBAN IN AFGHANISTAN AND CONSIDERED HEAD OF STATE.

MULLAH OMAR* CONDEMNS THIS ACT...

AND OSAMA IS NOT RESPONSIBLE. WE WANT PEACE IN ALL COUNTRIES.

EVIDENCE OF BIN LADEN'S ROLE KEPT POURING IN...

INCLUDING LINKS TO A FLIGHT SCHOOL IN FLORIDA WHERE MOHAMED ATTA AND MARWAN AL SHEHHI, SUSPECTED TERRORISTS, TOOK LESSONS.

ONE DAY LATER, THE PRESIDENT LABELED THE ATTACKS "ACTS OF WAR."

HE BEGAN WORKING TO FORGE AN INTERNATIONAL COALITION SUPPORTING A MILITARY RESPONSE-- ONCE THE ENEMY WAS IDENTIFIED.

MEANWHILE, A SENIOR TALIBAN SPOKESMAN CLAIMED THAT BIN LADEN WAS NOT INVOLVED IN THE TERRORIST ATTACKS OF SEPTEMBER 11.

HE DOES NOT HAVE SUCH CAPABILITIES.

SECRETARY OF STATE COLIN POWELL ALSO WORKED TO PERSUADE FOREIGN GOVERNMENTS TO JOIN IN THE AMERICAN RESPONSE, WARNING THEM THAT THEY COULD NO LONGER REMAIN NEUTRAL IN THIS WAR AGAINST TERRORISM.

AND THE TALIBAN WILL NOT BE FOUND GUILTY OF SUCH COWARDLY ACTS.

CONGRESS IMMEDIATELY MOVED TO GIVE THE ADMINISTRATION $40 BILLION TO WAGE ITS ANTITERRORISM INITIATIVE.

AND DEFENSIVE MEASURES CONTINUED WITH PLANES BEING GROUNDED, KEY BUILDINGS BEING EVACUATED, AND POSSIBLE TERRORISTS BEING TAKEN INTO CUSTODY.

ON SEPTEMBER 14, THREE DAYS AFTER THE ATTACKS, THE SENATE VOTED 98-0 TO GIVE PRESIDENT BUSH THE POWER TO USE "ALL NECESSARY AND APPROPRIATE FORCE" TO RESPOND TO THE ATTACKS.

THE HOUSE CHIMED IN WITH A 420-1 VOTE.

THE PRESIDENT IMMEDIATELY RESPONDED, GIVING THE PENTAGON THE RIGHT TO CALL UP 50,000 RESERVISTS, AND WARNED THE MILITARY TO GET READY FOR A LONG WAR AGAINST TERRORISM.

WE'RE AT *WAR!* THERE'S BEEN AN ACT OF WAR DECLARED UPON AMERICA BY TERRORISTS AND WE WILL RESPOND ACCORDINGLY.

THE PRESIDENT REPORTED THAT LEADERS OF PAKISTAN, INDIA, AND SAUDI ARABIA OFFERED "POSITIVE" SUPPORT AND THEN TOLD REPORTERS...

...THIS *CRUSADE,* THIS WAR ON TERROR, IS GOING TO TAKE A WHILE. WE WILL RID THE WORLD OF THE *EVILDOERS!*

A CBS/NY TIMES POLL, ANNOUNCED ON SEPTEMBER 15, SHOWED A VAST MAJORITY OF AMERICANS SUPPORTED THE WAR ON TERRORISM.

MEETING WITH CONGRESSIONAL LEADERS ON SEPTEMBER 18, 2001, ATTORNEY GENERAL JOHN ASHCROFT SUGGESTED AN EXPANSION OF THE JUSTICE DEPARTMENT'S USE OF WIRETAPS, COMPLAINING...

...IT'S EASIER TO INVESTIGATE SOMEONE ON ALLEGED GAMBLING SCHEMES THAN TO INVESTIGATE SOMEONE INVOLVED IN TERRORISM.

TELEPHONE SURVEILLANCE HAS BEEN LIMITED HISTORICALLY TO SPECIFIC TELEPHONES RATHER THAN TO PEOPLE.

ON SEPTEMBER 17, WHILE PAKISTANI OFFICIALS PURPORTEDLY TOLD THE TALIBAN THAT SURRENDERING BIN LADEN COULD SPARE AFGHANISTAN FROM AMERICAN ATTACK...

...PRESIDENT BUSH TOLD THE NATION TO PREPARE FOR U.S. MILITARY CASUALTIES IN THE ENSUING WAR ON TERRORISM. HE SAID HE WANTED OSAMA BIN LADEN... *DEAD OR ALIVE!* "WE WILL WIN THE WAR AND THERE WILL BE COSTS!"

ONE DAY LATER, TALIBAN LEADER MOHAMMED OMAR TOLD PAKISTAN'S INTELLIGENCE CHIEF, GEN. MAHMUD AHMED... "OSAMA WILL BE THE LAST PERSON TO LEAVE AFGHANISTAN."

U.S. AIR FORCE

IN ITS FIRST CONCRETE STEP TOWARD GOING TO WAR, AMERICAN MILITARY AIRPLANES LEFT THE U.S. FOR BASES OVERSEAS.

AN AIR FORCE OFFICER WAS QUOTED AS SAYING...

IT'S GOING TO BE *BIG!* THE PRESIDENT HAS TO DECIDE *HOW* BIG.

ON SEPTEMBER 20, THE PRESIDENT TOLD A JOINT MEETING OF CONGRESS... "THEY WILL HAND OVER THE TERRORISTS, OR THEY WILL SHARE THEIR FATE! ANY NATION THAT CONTINUES TO HARBOR OR SUPPORT TERRORISM WILL BE REGARDED AS A HOSTILE REGIME."

TO HELP PREVENT FURTHER ATTACKS AGAINST AMERICA, GOV. TOM RIDGE OF PENNSYLVANIA WAS CHOSEN ON SEPTEMBER 20 TO SERVE IN THE NEW POSITION OF SECRETARY OF HOMELAND SECURITY.

HE WAS CHARGED WITH COORDINATING THE EFFORTS OF U.S. DOMESTIC AND FOREIGN INTELLIGENCE AGENCIES, MANY RELUCTANT TO CONCEDE THE NEW DEPARTMENT'S OVERSIGHT.

ON SEPTEMBER 24, THE PRESIDENT FROZE ALL ASSETS IN THE U.S. OF SUSPECTED ISLAMIST TERRORIST GROUPS AND GAVE THE TREASURY SECRETARY AUTHORIZATION TO IMPOSE SANCTIONS ON BANKS, DOMESTIC AND FOREIGN, THAT PROVIDED FUNDS TO TERRORISTS. HE ALSO APPROVED AMERICAN SUPPORT IN ARMING ANTI-TALIBAN FORCES.

THE LATEST *NEW YORK TIMES*/CBS POLL TRACKS THE PRESIDENT'S APPROVAL RATING:

| SEPT.: 89% |
| AUG.: ABOUT 50% |
| JULY: ABOUT 55% |

ATTORNEY GENERAL ASHCROFT ON SEPTEMBER 24 CLAIMED THAT 352 PEOPLE HAD BEEN ARRESTED OR DETAINED AS POSSIBLE TERRORISTS OR CONSPIRATORS.
HE ALSO SAID THAT AN ADDITIONAL 392 WERE BEING SOUGHT FOR QUESTIONING.

ON SEPTEMBER 25, DEFENSE SECRETARY DONALD RUMSFELD RENAMED THE WAR AGAINST TERRORISM. THE ORIGINAL NAME, OPERATION INFINITE JUSTICE, WAS DISCARDED FOR HAVING UPSET ISLAMIC SENSIBILITIES. IT WOULD NOW BE KNOWN AS...

...OPERATION ENDURING FREEDOM!

THE PRESIDENT ON SEPTEMBER 27 ANNOUNCED THAT THE FEDERAL GOVERNMENT WOULD TAKE ON A LARGER ROLE IN AIRPORT SECURITY, ORDERING 4,000 NATIONAL GUARD TROOPS TO START PROTECTING THE NATION'S 420 AIRPORTS.

"THE TRAVELING PUBLIC WILL KNOW," HE SAID, "THAT WE ARE SERIOUS ABOUT AIRLINE SAFETY."

THEY *PASSED* THE RESOLUTION!

UNITE!

SAY NO

SAY NO

ACT NOW!

ON SEPTEMBER 28, THE UN SECURITY COUNCIL UNANIMOUSLY ADOPTED AN AMERICAN-SPONSORED RESOLUTION INSTRUCTING ALL UN MEMBERS TO CUT ALL POLITICAL, MILITARY, AND FINANCIAL CONNECTIONS WITH TERRORIST ORGANIZATIONS.

TWO DAYS LATER, THE PRESIDENT APPROVED A CONFIDENTIAL PLAN GIVING AID TO VARIOUS GROUPS OPPOSING THE TALIBAN IN AFGHANISTAN...

...WHILE THAT SAME DAY, ATTORNEY GENERAL ASHCROFT, FACING BIPARTISAN RESISTANCE, PRESSED CONGRESS FOR WIDER POWERS TO BATTLE DOMESTIC TERRORISM. SPEAKING ON *FACE THE NATION*, HE SAID...

TALK WILL NOT PREVENT TERRORISM. WE NEED TO HAVE ACTION BY CONGRESS.

UNITED STATES CONGRESS

WE NEED THE TOOLS TO PREVENT TERRORISM.

FARAH ★ QANDAHAR

THROUGH THE EARLY DAYS OF OCTOBER, SEVERAL EVENTS MOVED THE U.S. CLOSER TO WAR...

NATO REPORTED THAT THE U.S. HAD GIVEN "CLEAR AND COMPELLING PROOF" THAT BIN LADEN WAS BEHIND THE 9/11 ATTACKS.

THIS WAS APPARENT APPROVAL FOR AMERICAN ACTION AGAINST AL QAEDA.

AFGHANISTAN

KABUL

QANDAHAR

THE PENTAGON STATED THAT IT HAD DESIGNED A WAR PLAN AGAINST AFGHANISTAN USING BASES IN CENTRAL ASIA AND THE PERSIAN GULF.

SECRETARY RUMSFELD VISITED THE MIDDLE EAST TO PERSUADE COUNTRIES TO JOIN AMERICA'S ANTITERRORISM EFFORT.

AGAINST LITTLE OPPOSITION, U.S. PLANES AND MISSILES CONTINUED THEIR HEAVY BOMBARDMENT OF TALIBAN AND AL QAEDA POSITIONS IN AFGHANISTAN THROUGHOUT THE WEEK.
AMERICAN OFFICIALS CLAIMED THAT AT LEAST SEVEN OF THE COUNTRY'S LARGEST TRAINING CAMPS HAD BEEN DESTROYED.
THE NEXT PHASE, SAID A PENTAGON OFFICIAL, WOULD BE THE DISPATCH OF A SIGNIFICANT NUMBER OF GROUND TROOPS TO THE MIDDLE EAST AND CENTRAL ASIA.
"THEY WILL START TO GO," HE SAID, "BUT IT'S NOT BECAUSE WE HAVE A CLEAR AND DEFINED PLAN. BUT NOTHING HAS BEEN RULED OUT."

IN A LETTER TO THE UNITED NATIONS, U.S. AMBASSADOR JOHN NEGROPONTE LABELED THE BOMBING ATTACKS ACTS OF SELF-DEFENSE. AND PRESIDENT BUSH ON OCTOBER 11 SAID THE ATTACKS WOULD GO ON...

...FOR AS LONG AS IT TAKES!

PRESIDENT OF THE UNITE

A NUMBER OF ANTHRAX-LACED LETTERS ARE MAILED FROM TRENTON, NJ, TO VARIOUS MEDIA OUTLETS JUST A WEEK AFTER 9/11, THE FIRST BEING OPENED IN FLORIDA. THE FBI AND HEALTH OFFICIALS, HOWEVER, FIND NO CONNECTION BETWEEN THE TWO ACTS OF TERROR.

WITHIN DAYS OF SEPTEMBER 11, SOME OFFICIALS, INCLUDING THE PRESIDENT, WONDERED IF SADDAM HUSSEIN, IRAQ'S TYRANNICAL RULER, WAS INVOLVED IN THE ATTACKS. MANY, INCLUDING COUNTERTERRORISM EXPERT RICHARD CLARKE, FOUND NO SUBSTANTIATING EVIDENCE.

UZBEKISTAN, A FORMER SOVIET REPUBLIC, AGREED TO ALLOW THE U.S. THE USE OF ITS AIR BASES FOR A PROMISE OF PROVIDING SECURITY.

ON OCTOBER 12, IT WAS REPORTED THAT ALMOST 1,000 AMERICAN TROOPS WERE ALREADY ENCAMPED AT AN AIRFIELD CLOSE TO THE AFGHAN BORDER.

ON THE HOME FRONT, LAW OFFICIALS CLAIMED ON OCTOBER 14 THAT THEIR RECENT AGGRESSIVE CAMPAIGN OF ARRESTS HAD DESTROYED SEVERAL AL QAEDA CELLS.

AT LEAST TEN OF 700 ARRESTED, THEY SAID, WERE LINKED TO THE TERRORIST ORGANIZATION.

AFTER TEN DAYS OF U.S. BOMBARDMENT, A SENIOR TALIBAN LEADER, IN SECRET PAKISTANI CONFERENCES, ASKED FOR A PAUSE WHILE MODERATE MEMBERS OF THE TALIBAN TRIED TO PERSUADE THEIR SUPREME LEADER, MULLAH MOHAMMED OMAR, TO HAND OVER BIN LADEN.

BUT PRESIDENT BUSH REJECTED EVERY OFFER. HE WAS QUOTED AS SAYING...

ALL THEY'VE GOT TO DO IS TURN HIM OVER, AND HIS COLLEAGUES, AND THE THUGS HE HIDES.

"NOT ONLY TURN HIM OVER, TURN THE AL QAEDA ORGANIZATION OVER, DESTROY ALL THE CAMPS--ACTUALLY WE'RE DOING A PRETTY GOOD JOB OF THAT RIGHT NOW--AND RELEASE THE HOSTAGES THEY HOLD. THERE IS NO NEGOTIATION...PERIOD."

A NEW PHASE IN THE WAR WITH AFGHANISTAN BEGAN ON OCTOBER 19. MORE THAN 100 U.S. ARMY RANGERS AND OTHER SPECIAL FORCES WERE DROPPED BY HELICOPTER IN A RAID FROM A BASE IN PAKISTAN TO MILITARY TARGETS NEAR KANDAHAR, AFGHANISTAN'S SECOND-LARGEST CITY. TWO U.S. MILITARY PERSONNEL WERE KILLED IN AN ACCIDENT RELATED TO THIS MISSION, WHICH WAS THE START OF DIRECT COMBAT.

SHRRAK!

AS THESE OPERATIONS CONTINUED, ON OCTOBER 25, THE U.S. SENATE PASSED A SWEEPING ANTITERRORISM BILL, EXPANDING THE GOVERNMENT'S RIGHT TO USE ELECTRONIC SURVEILLANCE, RESTRAIN IMMIGRANTS, AND HAMPER MONEY-LAUNDERING BANKS. THIS WAS KNOWN LATER AS THE PATRIOT ACT.

TWO DAYS LATER, U.S. WARPLANES CARRIED OUT THEIR FIRST IMPORTANT RAID ON FRONT-LINE TALIBAN TROOPS NEAR KABUL, THE CAPITAL.

MEANWHILE, THE CZECH INTERIOR MINISTER CLAIMED ON OCTOBER 26 THAT AN IRAQI INTELLIGENCE OFFICIAL MET WITH TERRORIST LEADER MOHAMED ATTA FIVE MONTHS BEFORE THE 9/11 ATTACKS.

BLAM! BRAM!

ON OCTOBER 27, ADMIRAL SIR MICHAEL BOYCE, CHIEF OF THE BRITISH DEFENSE STAFF, SAID HE BELIEVED THIS AFGHAN EXPEDITION WAS "THE MOST DIFFICULT OPERATION EVER UNDERTAKEN BY THIS COUNTRY POST-KOREA."

IT WAS NOT GOING TO BE A SHORT WAR.

ITS ORIGINS STILL A MYSTERY, THE ANTHRAX FEAR CONTINUES THROUGH THE MONTH OF OCTOBER AS ENVELOPES OF THE POISON ARE MAILED TO THE SENATE, CAPITOL HILL, AND SEVERAL NEW YORK OFFICES. ULTIMATELY, 22 PEOPLE DEVELOP ANTHRAX INFECTIONS AND 5 DIE.

ON OCTOBER 30, A SMALL NUMBER OF U.S. TROOPS WERE REPORTED TO HAVE BEEN IN AFGHANISTAN FOR SEVERAL DAYS, AIDING THE NORTHERN ALLIANCE IN ITS BATTLE WITH THE TALIBAN. TILL THEN, THE NORTHERN ALLIANCE--A COLLECTION OF NON-PASHTUN ETHNIC GROUPS--HAD FOUGHT ALONE AGAINST THE TALIBAN.

DEFENSE SECRETARY RUMSFELD SAID THE U.S. TROOPS WERE THERE HELPING TO FORM SUPPLY ROUTES, TO BETTER COMMUNICATIONS, AND TO POINT OUT TALIBAN TARGETS FOR AIR STRIKES.

SANDSTORMS, SEVERE FOG, AND ICY WEATHER IN LATE OCTOBER AND EARLY NOVEMBER HINDERED U.S. HELICOPTERS FROM FLYING, KEPT AMERICAN COMMANDO MISSIONS TO A MINIMUM, AND SLOWED ANY ADVANCE BY THE NORTHERN ALLIANCE.

MEANWHILE, U.S. GOVERNMENT MEDICAL OFFICIALS WERE PREPARING FOR POSSIBLE TERRORIST-CAUSED OUTBREAKS OF SMALL-POX, AND WERE STILL BAFFLED BY WHO COULD BE CAUSING THE ANTHRAX SCARES.

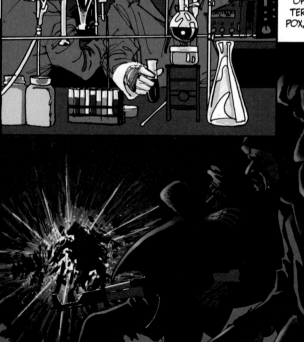

AT LAST, BY THE MIDDLE OF NOVEMBER, AIDED BY CONTINUOUS HEAVY U.S. BOMBARDMENT, REBEL FORCES MOVED FIRST NORTHWARD, CAPTURING THE PRIZED CITY OF MAZAR-I-SHARIF, THEN SOUTHWARD TOWARD KABUL.

OFFICIALS IN CONGRESS AND THE ADMINISTRATION EXPECTED COSTS IN AFGHANISTAN TO BE MORE THAN $1 BILLION A MONTH AND THEN TO RISE RAPIDLY.

DESPITE WARNINGS BY THE U.S. AND PAKISTAN TO STAY OUT OF KABUL, THE NORTHERN ALLIANCE ROLLED INTO THE CAPITAL ON NOVEMBER 13 WITH TANKS TRUCKS, AND TROOP CARRIERS, WHILE THE TALIBAN RETREATED.

INITIALLY, NORTHERN ALLIANCE TROOPS WERE GREETED JOYOUSLY BY THE CITIZENRY, SOME WOMEN BRIEFLY EXPOSING THEIR FACES THOUGH KEEPING ON THEIR BURKAS.

BACKGROUND

AFGHANISTAN HAS A MULTIETHNIC CULTURE. HISTORICALLY, THE NATION HAS BEEN MADE UP OF A LOOSE FEDERATION OF TRIBES AND ETHNIC GROUPS UNDER A WEAK CENTRAL GOVERNMENT IN KABUL. WHO ARE THESE GROUPS?

PASHTUNS--THOUGH NOT A MAJORITY, THE LARGEST GROUP ARE THE PASHTUNS, WHO MAKE UP ABOUT 40% OF THE POPULACE AND HAVE LONG CONTROLLED EVENTS.

INTERIM PRESIDENT HAMID KARZAI BELONGS TO THE POPULAZI CLAN, WHICH IS PART OF THE PASHTUN TRIBE. LIKE MOST GROUPS, THEY SUFFERED DISCRIMINATION WHEN MEMBERS WERE FORCIBLY MOVED TO THE NORTH ABOUT A CENTURY AGO. PASHTUNS ARE GENERALLY SUNNI MUSLIMS.

HAZARAS--THE SHIA MUSLIM HAZARAS MAKE UP ABOUT 19% OF THE NATION. THEY HAD SUFFERED RELIGIOUS DISCRIMINATION FROM THE TALIBAN, WHO ARE HARD-LINE SUNNIS.

TAJIKS--ABOUT 25% OF THE POPULATION. THEY WERE A LEADING COMPONENT OF THE NORTHERN ALLIANCE AND WERE REPUTED TO HAVE MASSACRED HAZARAS. THEY MAKE UP THE BULK OF AFGHANISTAN'S EDUCATIONAL ELITE AND WIELD IMPORTANT POLITICAL POWER.

TAJIKS ARE MOSTLY SUNNI MUSLIMS WHO SPEAK PERSIAN AND LIVE PREDOMINANTLY IN THE NORTHEAST AND WEST.

UZBEKS--A TURKIC GROUP, MAKE UP 6% OF THE AFGHAN POPULATION AND ARE SUNNI MUSLIMS.

THERE ARE MANY OTHER SMALLER GROUPS, INCLUDING THE TURKMEN, AIMAQ, BALUK, AND NURISTANIS.

TURKMEN

TAJIK

AIMAQ

UZBEK

PASHTUN

HAZARA

WITH THE ROUT OF THE TALIBAN IN THE NORTH, AMERICAN COMMANDOS--IN NUMBERS OF ABOUT A HUNDRED--LANDED IN SOUTH AFGHANISTAN TO CARRY OUT COVERT OPERATIONS. THIS INCLUDED BLOCKING ROADS, BLOWING UP BRIDGES, AND MARKING TARGETS AND POTENTIAL LANDING PLACES.

THE VICTORIOUS NORTHERN ALLIANCE GAVE UP ITS EXCLUSIVE POWER IN KABUL TO ALLOW A TRANSITIONAL GOVERNMENT THAT WOULD BE "BROAD-BASED, MULTIETHNIC, AND FULLY REPRESENTATIVE."

TALK OF IRAQ CONTINUED AS NATIONAL SECURITY ADVISER CONDOLEEZZA RICE SAID ON CNN...

WE HAVE SAID FOR A NUMBER OF YEARS THAT IRAQ IS A THREAT TO ITS NEIGHBORS, TO ITS PEOPLE, TO THE REGION, AND TO AMERICAN INTERESTS.

WE'LL DEAL WITH THAT SITUATION EVENTUALLY.

THE OFFICIAL COUNT OF THE DEAD AND MISSING FROM THE 9/11 ATTACKS IN NYC WAS ANNOUNCED, AND IT FELL, THANKFULLY, TO BELOW 3,900. THIS WAS 3,000 FEWER THAN OFFICIALS HAD FEARED.

17

IN AFGHANISTAN, HUNDREDS OF U.S. MARINES LANDED NEAR THE SOUTHERN CITY OF KANDAHAR ON NOVEMBER 25...

IT WAS THE FIRST MAJOR INFUSION OF AMERICAN TROOPS IN THAT NATION.

...WHILE THE NORTHERN ALLIANCE REPORTED THE CAPTURE OF KUNDUZ, THE LAST TALIBAN STRONG-HOLD IN THE NORTH.

WHILE A REPORTED 500 MARINES DUG IN NEAR KANDAHAR, PRESIDENT BUSH CALLED ON IRAQI PRESIDENT SADDAM HUSSEIN TO READMIT UN ARMS INSPECTORS TO VERIFY THAT HE WAS NOT DEVELOPING WEAPONS OF MASS DESTRUCTION.

WHAT ACTIONS WOULD BE TAKEN IF HE REFUSES?

HE'LL FIND OUT!

SECRETARY OF STATE COLIN POWELL AT THAT TIME SAID THERE WAS NO EVIDENCE LINKING SADDAM TO THE 9/11 ATTACKS.

THE FIRST AMERICAN DEATH OF THE WAR WAS REPORTED ON NOVEMBER 29: CIA OFFICER JOHNNY SPANN, 32, WAS KILLED BY REBELLIOUS TALIBAN PRISONERS.

ON THE HOME FRONT, AMERICAN OFFICIALS CLAIMED THAT ONLY A HANDFUL OF OVER 1,200 ARRESTED SINCE 9/11 HAD ANY CONNECTION TO TERRORISM.

ABOUT 600 OF THOSE IN CUSTODY WERE THERE FOR IMMIGRATION VIOLATIONS OR SIMILAR CRIMES.

BY EARLY DECEMBER, WITH BETWEEN 1,500 AND 2,000 AMERICAN TROOPS IN AFGHANISTAN, THE COMBINED MIGHT OF AFGHAN FORCES AND CONSTANT U.S. BOMBARDMENTS PUT THE TALIBAN ON THE EDGE OF COLLAPSE.

AN ERRANT U.S. BOMB, HOWEVER, CAUSED THE DEATHS OF THREE AMERICAN GI'S ON DECEMBER 6, THE FIRST U.S. SOLDIERS KILLED IN THE AFGHAN WAR.

KA-BLAM!

ON THAT SAME DAY, THE FIVE YEARS OF TALIBAN RULE ESSENTIALLY ENDED AS THE TALIBAN SURRENDERED.

AND THREE DAYS LATER, HAMID KARZAI, DESIGNATED LEADER OF THE INTERIM GOVERNMENT, ARRIVED IN KANDAHAR.

CHAPTER 3

VICTORY?

NINE WEEKS AFTER THE U.S. BOMBING CAMPAIGN BEGAN IN AFGHANISTAN, THE DEFENSE DEPARTMENT CLAIMED VICTORY OVER THE TALIBAN.

DEPUTY DEFENSE SECRETARY PAUL WOLFOWITZ SAID ON DECEMBER 10 THAT THE RAIDS HAD DISRUPTED AL QAEDA'S ABILITY TO COMMUNICATE AND DIMINISHED BIN LADEN'S AUTHORITY. HE ADDED... "THE WAR IN AFGHANISTAN IS NOT WON...THE AMERICAN PEOPLE HAVE TO BE PREPARED FOR THE FACT THAT WE MAY BE HUNTING TALIBAN AND AL QAEDA IN AFGHANISTAN MONTHS FROM NOW."

51% | 49%

A *NEW YORK TIMES*/CBS POLL ANNOUNCED ON DECEMBER 12... 51% OPPOSED TRYING FOREIGNERS ACCUSED OF TERRORISM IN SECRET MILITARY PROCEEDINGS.

80% | 20%

80% BELIEVED THE PRESIDENT SHOULD MAKE CHANGES IN THE JUSTICE SYSTEM IN CONSULTATION WITH CONGRESS, AND NOT BY EXECUTIVE ORDER.

A TAPE WAS RELEASED THE FOLLOWING DAY BY THE U.S. SHOWING OSAMA BIN LADEN BOASTING ABOUT THE 9/11 ATTACKS... "WE CALCULATED IN ADVANCE THE NUMBER OF CASUALTIES OF THE ENEMY WHO WOULD BE KILLED BASED ON THE POSITION OF THE TOWER..."

IN LATE DECEMBER, ADNAN IHSAN SAEED AL-HAIDERI, AN IRAQI DEFECTOR AND CIVIL ENGINEER, REPORTED TO U.S. OFFICIALS IN BANGKOK THAT HE HAD WORKED ON BIOLOGICAL, CHEMICAL, AND NUCLEAR WEAPONS IN SECRET IRAQI UNDER-GROUND WELLS AS RECENTLY AS A YEAR AGO.

...I WAS THE MOST OPTIMISTIC OF THEM ALL.

I HAVE COPIES OF MY CONTRACTS AND I CAN GIVE YOU COMPLETE DETAILS OF THESE PROJECTS.

THE ADMINISTRATION CITED THIS AS PROOF OF BIN LADEN'S GUILT IN CAUSING THE ATTACKS.

AMERICAN INTELLIGENCE OFFICIALS POINT OUT THAT IRAQI DEFECTORS MAY EMBELLISH THEIR STORIES TO GAIN ENTRY INTO THE U.S.

GOVERNMENT OFFICIALS HAVE FOUND NO EVIDENCE TO BACK UP EARLY SUSPICIONS THAT ANTHRAX STRAINS HAD COME FROM IRAQ. NO LIKELY SUSPECT HAS EMERGED.

ON DECEMBER 22, HAMID KARZAI--THE STRONG PASHTUN LEADER FROM KANDAHAR, WHO HAD FOUGHT THE SOVIET ARMIES AS DIRECTOR OF OPERATIONS OF THE AFGHAN NATIONAL LIBERATION FRONT--WAS INAUGURATED IN KABUL AS CHAIRMAN OF THE INTERIM GOVERNMENT IN AFGHANISTAN.

IN A PROMISING SHOW OF UNITY, MORE THAN 2,000 PEOPLE ATTENDED THE CEREMONY, INCLUDING GEN. TOMMY FRANKS, COMMANDER OF THE U.S.-LED CAMPAIGN AGAINST THE TALIBAN, AS WELL AS VARIOUS AFGHANI LEADERS.

DURING A FLIGHT FROM PARIS TO MIAMI, AIRPLANE PASSENGER RICHARD C. REID TRIED TO SET FIRE TO THE TONGUE OF HIS SNEAKER AND IGNITE THE EXPLOSIVES HIDDEN INSIDE. PASSENGERS AND CREW MEMBERS TACKLED THE 6'4" REID BEFORE IT COULD BE ACCOMPLISHED. A CONVERT TO ISLAM, REID'S MOTIVES WERE OBSCURE.

ON JANUARY 4, 2002, IT WAS ANNOUNCED THAT ARMY SPECIAL FORCES SERGEANT NATHAN ROSS CHAPMAN, AGE 31, WAS THE FIRST AMERICAN SOLDIER KILLED BY HOSTILE FIRE IN AFGHANISTAN.

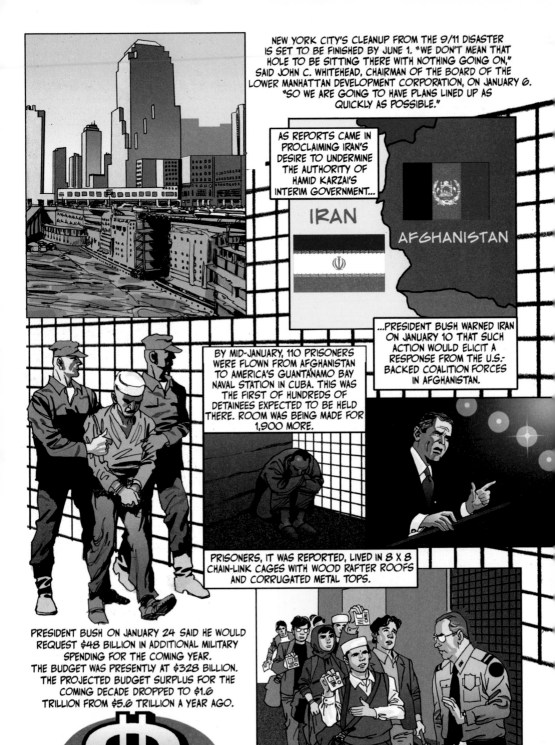

NEW YORK CITY'S CLEANUP FROM THE 9/11 DISASTER IS SET TO BE FINISHED BY JUNE 1. "WE DON'T MEAN THAT HOLE TO BE SITTING THERE WITH NOTHING GOING ON," SAID JOHN C. WHITEHEAD, CHAIRMAN OF THE BOARD OF THE LOWER MANHATTAN DEVELOPMENT CORPORATION, ON JANUARY 6. "SO WE ARE GOING TO HAVE PLANS LINED UP AS QUICKLY AS POSSIBLE."

AS REPORTS CAME IN PROCLAIMING IRAN'S DESIRE TO UNDERMINE THE AUTHORITY OF HAMID KARZAI'S INTERIM GOVERNMENT...

IRAN

AFGHANISTAN

...PRESIDENT BUSH WARNED IRAN ON JANUARY 10 THAT SUCH ACTION WOULD ELICIT A RESPONSE FROM THE U.S.-BACKED COALITION FORCES IN AFGHANISTAN.

BY MID-JANUARY, 110 PRISONERS WERE FLOWN FROM AFGHANISTAN TO AMERICA'S GUANTÁNAMO BAY NAVAL STATION IN CUBA. THIS WAS THE FIRST OF HUNDREDS OF DETAINEES EXPECTED TO BE HELD THERE. ROOM WAS BEING MADE FOR 1,900 MORE.

PRISONERS, IT WAS REPORTED, LIVED IN 8 X 8 CHAIN-LINK CAGES WITH WOOD RAFTER ROOFS AND CORRUGATED METAL TOPS.

PRESIDENT BUSH ON JANUARY 24 SAID HE WOULD REQUEST $48 BILLION IN ADDITIONAL MILITARY SPENDING FOR THE COMING YEAR. THE BUDGET WAS PRESENTLY AT $328 BILLION. THE PROJECTED BUDGET SURPLUS FOR THE COMING DECADE DROPPED TO $1.6 TRILLION FROM $5.6 TRILLION A YEAR AGO.

IMMIGRATION OFFICIALS ON JANUARY 27 CLAIMED THEY WERE AT LEAST A YEAR FROM REALIZING THEIR PROMISE TO TIGHTEN CONTROLS ON STUDENT VISAS, ENSURING SAFETY FROM TERRORISTS.

DAMMIT! I CAN'T GET THROUGH!

ON JANUARY 29, NEW YORK CITY FIRE DEPARTMENT OFFICIALS SAID THEY DID NOT HAVE ENOUGH RELIABLE COMMUNICATION EQUIPMENT TO KEEP TRACK OF FIREFIGHTERS ON 9/11 OR TO REACH THEM AS COLLAPSE BECAME IMMINENT. THE TRACKING SYSTEM, ORDERED SIX YEARS AGO BY CONGRESS, IS STILL IN THE TESTING STAGE, AND THE MANPOWER TO ENFORCE IT IS NOT THERE.

PRESIDENT BUSH DELIVERED HIS FIRST STATE OF THE UNION ADDRESS ON JANUARY 29, STATING THAT...

...OUR WAR AGAINST TERROR IS ONLY BEGINNING.

DESCRIBING IRAN, IRAQ, AND NORTH KOREA AS AN "AXIS OF EVIL," HE WENT ON TO DECLARE THAT ACTION WOULD BE TAKEN "IF DEEMED NECESSARY, NOT ONLY AGAINST TERRORISTS' ALLIES, BUT AGAINST ANY STATE DEVELOPING WEAPONS OF MASS DESTRUCTION."

CASTING THE PROPOSAL AS A WARTIME AGENDA, PRESIDENT BUSH SENT CONGRESS A $2.13 TRILLION BUDGET ON FEBRUARY 5 THAT FAVORED SPENDING ON MILITARY AND SECURITY PROGRAMS. IT ALSO CUT BACK ON SOCIAL PROGRAMS AND CONTINUED CUTTING TAXES. DEMOCRATS SAID THEY WOULD COOPERATE ON MATTERS PERTAINING TO THE FIGHT ON TERRORISM.

ON THE URGING OF SECRETARY OF STATE POWELL AND PRESSURE FROM EUROPEAN ALLIES, PRESIDENT BUSH AGREED THAT THE GENEVA CONVENTIONS WOULD APPLY TO TALIBAN CAPTIVES IN CUBA BUT NOT TO AL QAEDA DETAINEES.

SECRETARY OF STATE POWELL INFORMED THE SENATE BUDGET COMMITTEE ON FEBRUARY 12 THAT THE ADMINISTRATION WAS WEIGHING SEVERAL CHOICES FOR TOPPLING SADDAM HUSSEIN IN IRAQ. AS FAR AS IRAN AND NORTH KOREA, HE CLARIFIED, THERE WAS NO PLAN TO...

...START A WAR.

A NEW PHASE IN THE AFGHANISTAN WAR OPENED IN MID-FEBRUARY WHEN U.S. PLANES BOMBED MILITIA FORCES OPPOSED TO THE KARZAI GOVERNMENT. THESE WERE NEITHER MEMBERS OF THE TALIBAN NOR AL QAEDA.

THE CIA HAS WARNED THAT THE PRESENT CALM IN AFGHANISTAN COULD RETURN TO CHAOS IF THE VARIOUS WARLORDS AND ETHNIC GROUPS DO NOT GET TOGETHER AND CURB THEIR COMPETITIVE APPETITES.

PICTURE GALLERY

PASHTUNS ARE AN ETHNIC GROUP WHO LIVE IN EASTERN AND SOUTHERN AFGHANISTAN AND IN PROVINCES OF PAKISTAN.

THEY ARE THE MAIN ETHNIC GROUP OF THE TALIBAN.

A BURKA IS AN ALL-COVERING CLOAK, SOMETIMES WITH A VEIL, WORN BY SOME MUSLIM WOMEN.

TAJIKS ARE PERSIAN-SPEAKING PEOPLE OF IRANIAN ORIGIN LIVING IN CENTRAL ASIA. THE NORTHERN ALLIANCE ARE MAINLY ETHNIC TAJIKS, WHILE ALMOST 40% OF THE AFGHAN POPULATION AND MUCH OF PAKISTAN ARE PASHTUNS.

TOM DASCHLE

ROBERT C. BYRD

JOSEPH BIDEN

TRENT LOTT

TOM DELAY --
"DISGUSTING!"

LOTT--"[DASCHLE] SHOULD NOT BE TRYING TO DIVIDE OUR COUNTRY!"

AS FEBRUARY CAME TO A CLOSE, THREE DEMOCRATS QUESTIONED THE PRESIDENT'S STRATEGY IN THE WAR ON TERRORISM. MAJORITY LEADER TOM DASCHLE AND SENATOR ROBERT BYRD ASKED FOR A CLEARER UNDERSTANDING OF U.S. GOALS BEYOND STABILIZING AFGHANISTAN. SENATOR JOSEPH BIDEN COMPLAINED THAT NEITHER CONGRESS NOR OUR ALLIES WERE BEING SUFFICIENTLY CONSULTED. REPUBLICANS REPLIED...

THE WAR IN AFGHANISTAN WAS HARDLY OVER. IN SOME OF THE CONFLICT'S HEAVIEST FIGHTING, A MAJOR OFFENSIVE BY COALITION AND AFGHAN FORCES WAS LAUNCHED IN EARLY MARCH IN THE GARDEZ VALLEY AGAINST THE LAST STRONGHOLD OF AL QAEDA FORCES. AS U.S. WARPLANES CONDUCTED ROUND-THE-CLOCK BOMBINGS IN THE MOUNTAINOUS REGIONS NEAR ZORMAT, APPROXIMATELY 2,000 SOLDIERS, ABOUT HALF AFGHANS, FOUGHT ON THE GROUND.

DAYS LATER, 300 MORE U.S. TROOPS WERE ADDED TO THE BATTLE.

BY MARCH 18, AMERICAN COMMANDER GEN. TOMMY FRANKS CALLED OPERATIONS IN THE AREA AT AN END AND CALLED THIS LARGEST GROUND BATTLE OF THE WAR AN ABSOLUTE SUCCESS.

BUT BY THE END OF THE MONTH, THE SPRING THAW HAD ARRIVED AND AMERICAN OFFICIALS FEARED A RISE IN GUERRILLA ATTACKS.

AT THE END OF MARCH, THE ISRAELI GOVERNMENT DECLARES PALESTINIAN LEADER YASSER ARAFAT AN "ENEMY," AND WITH THE AID OF TANKS AND ARMORED VEHICLES ISOLATES HIM IN HIS RAMALLAH, PALESTINE, HEADQUARTERS.

REACTING TO RISING U.S. THREATS TO IRAQ, MEMBERS OF THE ARAB LEAGUE ON MARCH 28 WARNED THAT ANY ATTACK AGAINST IRAQ WOULD BE CONSIDERED AN ATTACK AGAINST ALL ARAB STATES...

...THAT WAS UNDERSCORED WITH A KISS BY CROWN PRINCE ABDULLAH OF SAUDI ARABIA ON THE FACE OF IRAQI REPRESENTATIVE IZZAT IBRAHIM.

IN EARLY APRIL, PAKISTANI PREMIER PERVEZ MUSHARRAF VISITED AFGHANISTAN AFTER YEARS OF TALIBAN SUPPORT AND AFTER REJECTING AMERICAN REQUESTS TO OPERATE IN PAKISTAN TO CAPTURE ESCAPING AL QAEDA FORCES. MUSHARRAF MET WITH INTERIM AFGHAN LEADER KARZAI TO GIVE HIM A $10 MILLION CHECK.

PRESIDENT BUSH ON APRIL 17 ENDORSED A MAJOR U.S.-LED INITIATIVE TO REBUILD AFGHANISTAN, WHICH HE COMPARED TO THE POST-WW II MARSHALL PLAN.

NEAR THE END OF THE MONTH, IT WAS REVEALED THAT THE FEDERAL EMERGENCY MANAGEMENT AGENCY (FEMA) HAD AWARDED LESS THAN $65 MILLION TO HELP NEEDY FAMILIES IN NEW YORK, A FRACTION OF THEIR USUAL AWARDS TO DISASTER VICTIMS.
THE AGENCY HAD DECIDED TO LIMIT PAYMENTS TO THOSE WHO COULD PROVE THEIR LOSSES WERE A "DIRECT RESULT" OF THE ATTACKS.

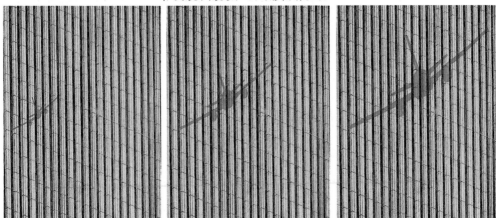

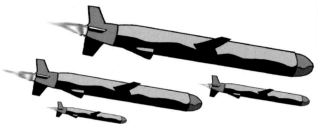

SENIOR ADMINISTRATION OFFICIALS TOLD *THE NEW YORK TIMES* ON APRIL 28 THAT THE ADMINISTRATION WAS CONSIDERING A PLAN TO DEPOSE IRAQI PRESIDENT SADDAM HUSSEIN BY USING A HUGE AIR CAMPAIGN AND A TROOP INVASION OF 70,000 TO 250,000. THE REPORTED INVASION WAS TO TAKE PLACE IN 2003, AND ACCORDING TO A DEFENSE DEPARTMENT OFFICIAL, IT WOULD "NOT LOOK LIKE WHAT WE DID IN AFGHANISTAN."

FEDERAL AUTHORITIES IN EARLY MAY CONCLUDED THAT THERE WAS NO EVIDENCE THAT TERRORIST MOHAMED ATTA MET WITH AN IRAQI INTELLIGENCE OFFICER BEFORE 9/11.

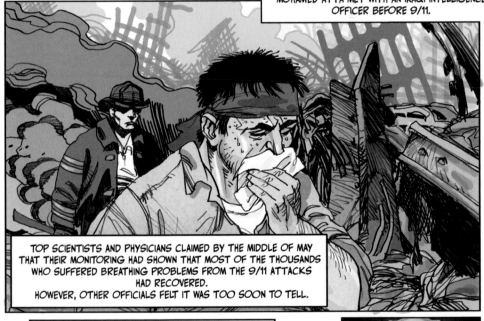

TOP SCIENTISTS AND PHYSICIANS CLAIMED BY THE MIDDLE OF MAY THAT THEIR MONITORING HAD SHOWN THAT MOST OF THE THOUSANDS WHO SUFFERED BREATHING PROBLEMS FROM THE 9/11 ATTACKS HAD RECOVERED.
HOWEVER, OTHER OFFICIALS FELT IT WAS TOO SOON TO TELL.

A NEW AFGHAN ARMY BEGAN TO TAKE SHAPE IN MID-MAY AS U.S. SPECIAL FORCES STARTED TRAINING THE FIRST 240 SOLDIERS FOR THE NATION.
OFFICIALS BELIEVE IT WILL TAKE TWO YEARS TO COMPLETE THE TASK.

SPEAKING FOR THE PRESIDENT ON MAY 15, PRESS SECRETARY ARI FLEISCHER SAID...

IT IS WIDELY KNOWN THAT WE HAD INFORMATION THAT BIN LADEN WANTED TO ATTACK THE UNITED STATES, [BUT] NOT FOR THE USE OF AN AIRPLANE AS A MISSILE.

IN MAY, HOWEVER, LAW ENFORCEMENT OFFICIALS ACKNOWLEDGED THAT THE FBI KNEW BY 1996 THAT AL QAEDA TERRORISTS MIGHT USE A PLANE IN A SUICIDE ATTACK AGAINST KEY GOVERNMENT BUILDINGS.

TAKE A LOOK AT THIS REPORT WE JUST RECEIVED!

SENATE MAJORITY LEADER TOM DASCHLE ON MAY 21 CALLED FOR AN INDEPENDENT COMMISSION TO STUDY WHAT THE GOVERNMENT KNEW AND WHAT ACTION IT TOOK PRIOR TO THE 9/11 ATTACKS.

I WOULD THINK THIS ESSENTIAL.

THE ADMINISTRATION AND CONGRESSIONAL REPUBLICANS, HOWEVER, APPEARED TO OPPOSE THE IDEA.

IN FACE OF STRONG CRITICISM FOR THE FBI'S PRE-9/11 INTELLIGENCE FAILURES, FBI DIRECTOR ROBERT MUELLER CONCEDED THERE WERE...

...DOTS THAT SHOULD HAVE BEEN CONNECTED.

HE ALSO STATED THAT HIS DEPARTMENT WOULD BE "REDESIGNED AND REFOCUSED," SHIFTING ITS MISSION FROM CRIME SOLVING TO THE PREVENTION OF FURTHER TERRORISM.

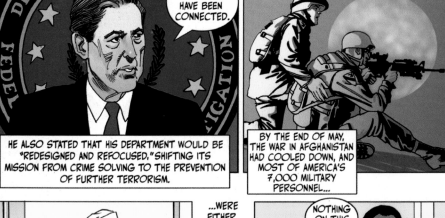

BY THE END OF MAY, THE WAR IN AFGHANISTAN HAD COOLED DOWN, AND MOST OF AMERICA'S 7,000 MILITARY PERSONNEL...

...WERE EITHER DRILLING, MOVING SUPPLIES, ADVISING, OR HELPING WITH RECON-STRUCTION PROJECTS.

NOTHING ON THIS GUY.

IN JUNE, THE CIA ADMITTED THAT THEY HAD LEARNED IN EARLY 2001 THAT KHALID AL-MIHDHAR, ONE OF THE 9/11 TERRORISTS, WAS LINKED TO A SUSPECT IN THE OCTOBER 12, 2000, BOMBING OF THE USS COLE IN THE YEMENI PORT OF ADEN.

THEY NEVER INFORMED THE FBI OR OTHER AGENCIES, AND HE WAS ALLOWED TO ENTER THE U.S.

FURTHER CRITICISM OF THE FBI WAS LEVELED BY FBI AGENT COLEEN ROWLEY, WHO HAD PREVIOUSLY WRITTEN CONGRESS IN MAY, BLAMING THE BUREAU FOR MISHANDLING THE INVESTIGATION OF ZACARIAS MOUSSAOUI, THE SUSPECTED 20TH HIJACKER.

IN EARLY JUNE, SHE TOLD A SENATE COMMITTEE THAT THE FBI BUREAUCRACY DISCOURAGED INNOVATION, DEMANDED TOO MUCH PAPERWORK, AND PUNISHED THOSE WHO SKIRTED RISK-AVERSE SUPERIORS.

> YOU ARE TO BE COMMENDED, AGENT ROWLEY, FOR THIS AND FOR YOUR EARLIER LETTER TO CONGRESS.

> FBI DIRECTOR MUELLER HAS PRAISED YOU AND ASSURES US THAT YOU FACE NEITHER RETALIATION NOR INTIMIDATION.

> THANK YOU, SENATOR.

ON JUNE 6, PRESIDENT BUSH ADDRESSED THE NATION AND CALLED FOR A CABINET-LEVEL DEPARTMENT COMBINING 22 FEDERAL AGENCIES INTO ONE ANTITERROR GROUP.

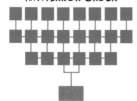

CONGRESS BEGAN DEBATING THE NECESSARY LEGISLATION.

SEVERAL DAYS LATER, SECRETARY OF DEFENSE RUMSFELD ACCUSED IRAQ OF PREPARING CHEMICAL WEAPONS AND DEVELOPING OFFENSIVE NUCLEAR AND BIOLOGICAL ARMS.

HE ALSO DESCRIBED SADDAM HUSSEIN AS A...

> ...WORLD-CLASS LIAR!

ON JUNE 13, AFGHANISTAN'S GRAND TRIBAL COUNCIL VOTED INTERIM LEADER KARZAI THE COUNTRY'S PRESIDENT FOR A TERM OF TWO YEARS.

ONE WEEK LATER HE WAS SWORN IN AND HIS CABINET APPROVED.

CRITICIZED FOR ITS DISTRIBUTION OF FUNDS TO NEW YORKERS HARMED BY THE 9/11 TRAGEDY, FEMA CHANGED ITS CRITERIA IN LATE JUNE. ANYONE WHO LIVED OR WORKED IN MANHATTAN AND HAD SUFFERED FINANCIALLY FROM THE ATTACK WOULD NOW BE ELIGIBLE.

AS WOULD ANYONE AFFECTED WHO HAD WORKED IN THE CITY'S OTHER BOROUGHS.

A U.S. AC-130 MISTAKENLY ATTACKED AN AFGHAN VILLAGE ON JULY 1, SHATTERING A WEDDING PARTY; UP TO 50 CIVILIANS WERE KILLED AND MORE THAN 120 WOUNDED. THE WHITE HOUSE OFFERED CONDOLENCES AS SHOCKED AFGHANS CRITICIZED THE RAID.

BRAK-A-TAK!

SCREECH!

IN EARLY JULY, AFGHAN VICE PRESIDENT HAJI ABDUL QADIR AND HIS DRIVER WERE SHOT AND KILLED NEAR HIS OFFICE IN KABUL BY GUNMEN WHO ESCAPED.

QADIR WAS ONE OF THE FEW PASHTUNS IN THE KARZAI GOVERNMENT DOMINATED BY TAJIKS.

AFTER FOUR YEARS OF BUDGET SURPLUSES, ON JULY 12, MITCH DANIELS, WHITE HOUSE OFFICE OF MANAGEMENT AND BUDGET DIRECTOR, ANNOUNCES A FEDERAL BUDGET DEFICIT OF $165 BILLION IN 2002. HE ALSO PREDICTS THAT THE DEFICIT WILL IMPROVE TO $109 BILLION BY NEXT YEAR, RETURNING TO A SURPLUS WITHIN TWO YEARS AFTER THAT.

BY LATE JULY, THE CONSTANT TALK IN THE U.S. OF OVERTHROWING SADDAM BY MILITARY MEANS ALARMED MANY EUROPEAN NATIONS. A FRENCH OFFICIAL IN PARIS SAID THAT SOME OF PRESIDENT BUSH'S AIDES WERE... "OBSESSED ABOUT IRAQ WHILE WE ARE OBSESSED ABOUT ACHIEVING PEACE."

AND TURKISH PRIME MINISTER BULENT ECEVIT PREDICTED THAT AMERICA WOULD FACE A LONG WAR IF THEY TRIED TO TOPPLE SADDAM.

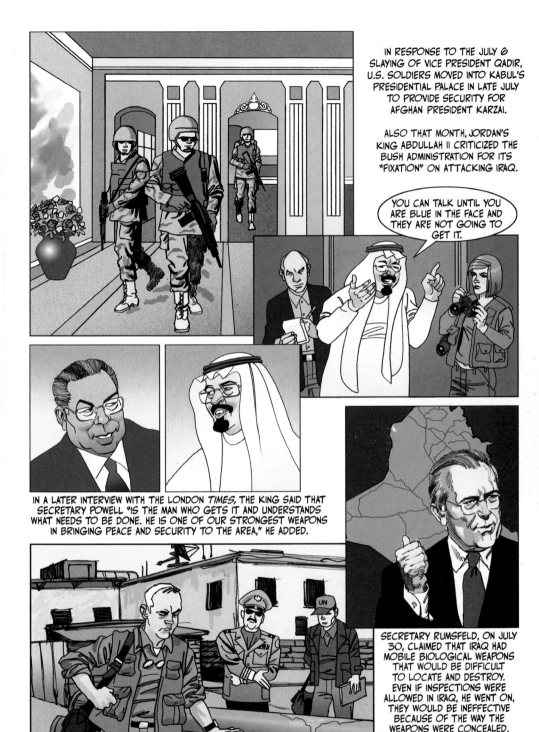

IN RESPONSE TO THE JULY 6 SLAYING OF VICE PRESIDENT QADIR, U.S. SOLDIERS MOVED INTO KABUL'S PRESIDENTIAL PALACE IN LATE JULY TO PROVIDE SECURITY FOR AFGHAN PRESIDENT KARZAI.

ALSO THAT MONTH, JORDAN'S KING ABDULLAH II CRITICIZED THE BUSH ADMINISTRATION FOR ITS "FIXATION" ON ATTACKING IRAQ.

YOU CAN TALK UNTIL YOU ARE BLUE IN THE FACE AND THEY ARE NOT GOING TO GET IT.

IN A LATER INTERVIEW WITH THE LONDON *TIMES*, THE KING SAID THAT SECRETARY POWELL "IS THE MAN WHO GETS IT AND UNDERSTANDS WHAT NEEDS TO BE DONE. HE IS ONE OF OUR STRONGEST WEAPONS IN BRINGING PEACE AND SECURITY TO THE AREA," HE ADDED.

SECRETARY RUMSFELD, ON JULY 30, CLAIMED THAT IRAQ HAD MOBILE BIOLOGICAL WEAPONS THAT WOULD BE DIFFICULT TO LOCATE AND DESTROY. EVEN IF INSPECTIONS WERE ALLOWED IN IRAQ, HE WENT ON, THEY WOULD BE INEFFECTIVE BECAUSE OF THE WAY THE WEAPONS WERE CONCEALED.

FACING MOUNTING INTERNATIONAL PRESSURE, IRAQ REVERSED ITS LONG-HELD REFUSAL TO ADMIT UN WEAPONS INSPECTORS. ON AUGUST 1, IRAQI OFFICIALS ASKED UN SECRETARY-GENERAL KOFI ANNAN TO SEND A TEAM TO BAGHDAD FOR DISCUSSIONS. BUT FOUR DAYS LATER, THE UN SECURITY COUNCIL AND THE SECRETARY-GENERAL REFUSED. INSPECTORS WOULD RETURN TO IRAQ ONLY IF SADDAM HUSSEIN AGREED TO ABIDE BY THE UN'S RULES OF INSPECTION.

SEVERAL TOP REPUBLICAN LEADERS IN MID-AUGUST SEEMED TO BREAK WITH THE PRESIDENT'S POSITION ON IRAQ. FORMER NATIONAL SECURITY ADVISER BRENT SCOWCROFT, IN *THE WALL STREET JOURNAL*, WARNED THAT AN ATTACK ON IRAQ WOULD JEOPARDIZE THE GLOBAL ANTITERRORISM CAMPAIGN. HENRY KISSINGER, IN THE *WASHINGTON POST*, DESCRIBED THE COMPLICATIONS INHERENT TO ANY MILITARY CAMPAIGN. AND SENATOR CHUCK HAGEL DECLARED THAT THE CIA HAS *"ABSOLUTELY NO EVIDENCE"* THAT IRAQ HAD OR WOULD SOON HAVE NUCLEAR WEAPONS.

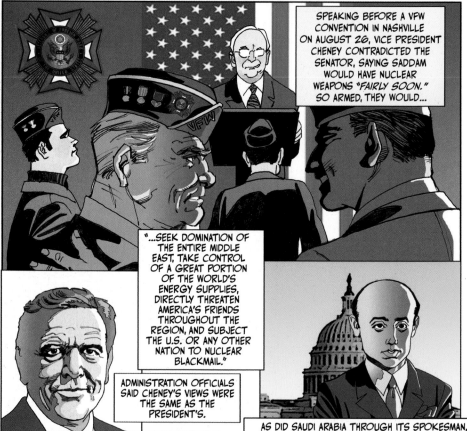

SPEAKING BEFORE A VFW CONVENTION IN NASHVILLE ON AUGUST 26, VICE PRESIDENT CHENEY CONTRADICTED THE SENATOR, SAYING SADDAM WOULD HAVE NUCLEAR WEAPONS *"FAIRLY SOON."* SO ARMED, THEY WOULD...

"...SEEK DOMINATION OF THE ENTIRE MIDDLE EAST, TAKE CONTROL OF A GREAT PORTION OF THE WORLD'S ENERGY SUPPLIES, DIRECTLY THREATEN AMERICA'S FRIENDS THROUGHOUT THE REGION, AND SUBJECT THE U.S. OR ANY OTHER NATION TO NUCLEAR BLACKMAIL."

ADMINISTRATION OFFICIALS SAID CHENEY'S VIEWS WERE THE SAME AS THE PRESIDENT'S.

GERMAN CHANCELLOR GERHARD SCHRÖDER IMMEDIATELY DISAPPROVED OF CHENEY'S SPEECH, CLAIMING IT WOULD UNDERMINE ANY CHANCE OF IRAQ AGREEING TO INSPECTIONS.

AS DID SAUDI ARABIA THROUGH ITS SPOKESMAN, ADEL AL-JUBEIR. "THERE IS A PROCESS UNDER WAY WITH THE UN TO BRING INSPECTORS BACK IN. IF SUCCESSFUL, WE CAN ACHIEVE OUR OBJECTIVES WITHOUT FIRING A SINGLE BULLET OR LOSING A SINGLE LIFE."

IN EARLY SEPTEMBER, AN AMERICAN SPECIAL OPERATIONS TEAM ASSIGNED TO GUARD AFGHAN PRESIDENT KARZAI IN KANDAHAR FOILED AN ASSASSINATION ATTEMPT.

BLAM! BLAM! BLAM!

AND IN KABUL, A HUGE CAR BOMB EXPLODED, KILLING 25 PEOPLE AND WOUNDING DOZENS OF OTHERS.

BRAMM!

THE WAR IN AFGHANISTAN WAS *NOT* OVER.

PRESIDENT BUSH UNSUCCESSFULLY CALLED ON THE LEADERS OF FRANCE, RUSSIA, AND CHINA TO SUPPORT A COALITION ARMY AGAINST IRAQ. BUT BRITISH PRIME MINISTER TONY BLAIR DECLARED AT CAMP DAVID, MARYLAND... "THE POLICY OF INACTION IS NOT A POLICY WE CAN RESPONSIBLY SUBSCRIBE TO." HE BECAME THE FIRST EUROPEAN LEADER TO SIDE WITH PRESIDENT BUSH'S HARD LINE WITH IRAQ.

A *NEW YORK TIMES/CBS* POLL ANNOUNCES ON SEPTEMBER 18 THAT ONE-QUARTER OF THE AMERICAN PUBLIC BELIEVES IRAQ PRESENTS A GRAVE THREAT THAT THE GOVERNMENT SHOULD CONFRONT NOW. TWO-THIRDS OF THE PUBLIC BELIEVES THAT THE NATION SHOULD WAIT FOR THE SUPPORT OF ALLIES.

TOP NATIONAL SECURITY ADVISERS MADE THE ADMINISTRATION'S CASE.

"TIME IS NOT ON OUR SIDE."

"WE DON'T WANT THE SMOKING GUN TO BE A MUSHROOM CLOUD."

"IMAGINE A SEPTEMBER 11 WITH WEAPONS OF MASS DESTRUCTION."

THE DAY AFTER, PRESIDENT BUSH ADDRESSED THE UN'S GENERAL ASSEMBLY. POINTING OUT THAT SADDAM HUSSEIN HAD IGNORED ELEVEN YEARS OF UN RESOLUTIONS MEANT TO FORCE IRAQ'S DISARMAMENT AND END HIS REPRESSION OF THE IRAQI PEOPLE, BUSH DECLARED THAT IF THIS CONTINUED...

...ACTION WILL BE UNAVOIDABLE!

MANY DELEGATES EXPRESSED RELIEF THAT PRESIDENT BUSH DECLARED HIS INTENT TO WORK WITH THE SECURITY COUNCIL IN FORCING IRAQ TO COMPLY.

IN MID-SEPTEMBER, RAMZI BIN AL-SHIBH, A SUSPECTED HIGH-RANKING AL QAEDA OPERATIVE, WAS CAPTURED BY A JOINT U.S.-PAKISTANI FORCE IN KARACHI.

THOUGHT TO BE AN ASSOCIATE OF MOHAMED ATTA AND A COCONSPIRATOR IN THE 9/11 PLOT, HE WAS AMONG A REPORTED TEN SUSPECTS CAPTURED.

UN SECRETARY-GENERAL KOFI ANNAN DECLARED THAT, IN RESPONSE TO INTERNATIONAL PRESSURE, IRAQ WAS READY TO ACCEPT UN WEAPONS INSPECTORS "WITHOUT CONDITIONS!"

BOTH THE U.S. AND BRITAIN EXPRESSED SKEPTICISM AND CONTINUED TO PRESSURE IRAQ.

THE ADMINISTRATION'S CHIEF ECONOMIC ADVISER, LAWRENCE B. LINDSEY, ESTIMATED THE COST OF WAR WITH IRAQ COULD BE AS HIGH AS $100 BILLION TO $200 BILLION. ON SEPTEMBER 19, PRESIDENT BUSH ASKED CONGRESS TO GRANT HIM FULL AUTHORITY TO EMPLOY... "ALL MEANS TO DISARM IRAQ AND DISLODGE SADDAM HUSSEIN--INCLUDING FORCE." IF THE UN DOES NOT HANDLE THIS PROBLEM, HE ADDED, "WE AND SOME OF OUR FRIENDS WILL."

ON SEPTEMBER 20, THE ADMINISTRATION GAVE IN TO CONGRESSIONAL DEMANDS FOR AN INDEPENDENT INVESTIGATION OF THE 9/11 ATTACKS.

IT WAS EXPECTED THAT THE BIPARTISAN PANEL WOULD SPEND MORE THAN A YEAR LOOKING INTO WHAT ACTIONS COULD HAVE PREVENTED THE ATTACKS.

ON SEPTEMBER 23, AL GORE, FORMER VICE PRESIDENT AND PRESIDENTIAL CANDIDATE, LASHED OUT AT PRESIDENT BUSH FOR WEAKENING THE WAR ON TERRORISM BY TURNING THE NATION'S ATTENTION TO SADDAM HUSSEIN. HE ADDED...

THE ADMINISTRATION HAS OPERATED IN A MANNER CALCULATED TO PLEASE THE PORTION OF ITS BASE THAT OCCUPIES THE FAR RIGHT.

THOUGH THE TALIBAN HAD BEEN DEPOSED AND A NEWLY ELECTED GOVERNMENT RULED AFGHANISTAN, POWERFUL WARLORDS CONTINUED TO BATTLE EACH OTHER IN THE NORTHERN PART OF THE COUNTRY.

TWO 4-STAR GENERALS APPEARED BEFORE THE SENATE ARMED SERVICES COMMITTEE AND WARNED THAT AN ATTACK ON IRAQ WITHOUT UN BACKING COULD LIMIT ALLIED AID, ENERGIZE AL QAEDA, AND HARM OUR DIPLOMATIC AND ECONOMIC INTEREST.

IT'S A QUESTION OF WHAT'S THE URGENCY HERE AND HOW SOON WOULD WE MEAN TO ACT UNILATERALLY.

THERE IS NOTHING THAT INDICATES THAT IN THE IMMEDIATE NEXT HOURS, NEXT DAYS, THERE'S GOING TO BE NUCLEAR-TIPPED MISSILES PUT ON LAUNCH PADS TO GO AGAINST OUR FORCES.

CLARK

SHALIKASHVILI

A BRITISH GOVERNMENT REPORT RELEASED ON SEPTEMBER 24 CLAIMED THAT IRAQ COULD LAUNCH BIOLOGICAL OR CHEMICAL WEAPONS IN 45 MINUTES.
IT ADDED THAT IRAQ WOULD HAVE NUCLEAR WEAPONS IN ONE TO FIVE YEARS.

IN LATE SEPTEMBER, IT WAS REVEALED THAT TERRORIST SUSPECT ZACARIAS MOUSSAOUI WAS ACCIDENTALLY GIVEN 48 CLASSIFIED FBI REPORTS INVOLVING THE BUREAU'S INVESTIGATION OF HIM AND AL QAEDA.

THEY WERE FOUND IN SEARCHES OF HIS PRISON CELL.

VERBAL DUELS CONTINUED FOR WEEKS BETWEEN AMERICAN AND IRAQI OFFICIALS AS THE UN SECURITY COUNCIL ATTEMPTED TO AGREE ON A RESOLUTION TO RESTART INSPECTIONS OF IRAQI WEAPONS FACILITIES.

[IRAQ HAS TRAINED MEMBERS OF AL QAEDA IN] BOMB MAKING, POISONS, AND DEADLY GASES. WE HAVE AN URGENT DUTY TO PREVENT THE WORST FROM HAPPENING!

THEIR REPORTS ARE A COLLECTION OF LIES. WE WILL NOT ACCEPT ANY NEW TERMS FOR UN INSPECTIONS.

FORMER PRESIDENT CLINTON SUPPORTED BUSH'S DESIRE FOR A STRONGLY WORDED RESOLUTION BUT WARNED, ON OCTOBER 2...

"PREEMPTIVE ACTION TODAY MAY COME BACK WITH UNWELCOME CONSEQUENCES IN THE FUTURE."

ON OCTOBER 10, THE PRESIDENT FINALLY WON AUTHORIZATION FROM CONGRESS--77-33 IN THE SENATE, 296-133 IN THE HOUSE--TO USE FORCE AGAINST IRAQ IF HE DEEMED IT NECESSARY.

THE OCTOBER 12 TERRORIST BOMBINGS IN BALI, INDONESIA, KILLED 202 PEOPLE AND WOUNDED 209.
THE PRESIDENT, WHO BELIEVED THE ATTACKS THE WORK OF AL QAEDA, COMMENTED...

"...I'M CONCERNED ABOUT OUR HOMELAND. IF I KNEW OF... A MOMENT OR A PLACE IN WHICH AN ENEMY WOULD ATTACK, WE'D DO A LOT ABOUT IT."

INDONESIAN DEFENSE MINISTER MATORI ABDUL DJALIL DECLARED, "THE BALI BOMB BLAST IS LINKED TO AL QAEDA WITH THE COOPERATION OF LOCAL TERRORISTS."

IN OCTOBER, SADDAM HUSSEIN RUNS UNOPPOSED IN IRAQ'S STATE-MANAGED PRESIDENTIAL ELECTION, WINNING 100% OF THE 11.4 MILLION VOTES. HE IS AWARDED A TERM OF SEVEN MORE YEARS. THAT SAME MONTH, CZECH PRESIDENT VÁCLAV HAVEL INFORMED THE BUSH ADMIN-ISTRATION THAT HE HAD FOUND *NO EVIDENCE* OF A SUPPOSED SECRET MEETING BETWEEN TERRORIST MOHAMED ATTA AND AN IRAQI INTELLIGENCE OFFICER BEFORE SEPTEMBER 11.

IN THE AMERICAN MIDTERM ELECTIONS, HELD NOVEMBER 5, THE REPUBLICANS WIN CONTROL OF THE SENATE AND A LARGER MAJORITY IN THE HOUSE; THE PRESIDENT'S POLITICAL POSITION IS CORRESPONDINGLY STRONGER.

ON NOVEMBER 8, AN AMERICAN RESOLUTION ON IRAQ GAINED UNANIMOUS APPROVAL IN THE SECURITY COUNCIL.
IT GAVE IRAQ A WEEK TO COMPLY WITH ITS DEMANDS AND 30 DAYS TO LIST ALL ITS NUCLEAR, CHEMICAL, AND BIOLOGICAL WEAPONS.
FIVE DAYS LATER, IRAQ, STILL DENYING IT HAD ANY WEAPONS OF MASS DESTRUCTION, AGREED TO ALLOW UN WEAPONS INSPECTORS TO START THEIR WORK.

IN LATE NOVEMBER, THE SENATE VOTED TO REORGANIZE 22 SEPARATE AGENCIES INTO A NEW DEPARTMENT OF HOMELAND SECURITY. THE PRESIDENT HAPPILY COMMENTED IN A CONFERENCE CALL TO REPUBLICAN SENATORS...

WE'RE MAKING GREAT PROGRESS IN THE WAR ON TERRORISM.

THIS IS A VERY IMPORTANT PIECE OF LEGISLATION. IT IS LANDMARK IN ITS SCOPE.

SIX DAYS LATER, HE SIGNED IT INTO LAW. THE FBI AND CIA WERE NOT AFFECTED, HOWEVER.

ON NOVEMBER 27, PRESIDENT BUSH NAMED HENRY KISSINGER CHAIRMAN OF THE INDEPENDENT COMMISSION INVESTIGATING THE 9/11 ATTACKS.
DEMOCRAT GEORGE MITCHELL WAS CHOSEN AS VICE CHAIRMAN.

HOWEVER, BOTH KISSINGER AND MITCHELL SOON RESIGNED, CITING CONFLICTS WITH EXISTING EMPLOYMENT.

IN EARLY DECEMBER, IRAQ GAVE THE UN A 12,000-PAGE DOCUMENT ALLEGEDLY SHOWING THAT IT HAD NO WEAPONS OF MASS DESTRUCTION OR PLANS TO DEVELOP THEM.
PRESIDENT BUSH DECLARED THAT THE DOCUMENT WOULD HAVE TO PASS AMERICAN SCRUTINY TO AVOID A MILITARY RESPONSE.

AFTER A FOUR-YEAR INTERRUPTION, THE UN ARMS INSPECTION TEAM STARTED WORK IN IRAQ ON NOVEMBER 27.
AFTER CHECKING THREE SITES FOR POSSIBLE TRACES OF BANNED WEAPONS, THEY REPORTED NO IRAQI INTERFERENCE.

A DAY BEFORE ACCEPTING THE NOBEL PEACE PRIZE IN OSLO THAT DECEMBER, FORMER PRESIDENT JIMMY CARTER SAID THAT IF THE UN FOUND THE IRAQIS IN COMPLIANCE...

...I SEE NO REASON FOR ARMED CONFLICT.

BY LATE DECEMBER 2002, A YEAR SINCE HAMID KARZAI HAD BEEN MADE PRESIDENT, THERE WAS A SENSE OF STABILITY IN AFGHANISTAN.

MORE THAN 15 MONTHS AFTER THE 9/11 ATTACKS, ONLY $5 BILLION HAD BEEN AWARDED TO NEW YORK CITY, LESS THAN A QUARTER OF THE $21.4 BILLION THE FEDERAL GOVERNMENT HAD PROMISED IN FINANCIAL ASSISTANCE.

THOUGH ADMITTING SEVERAL PROBLEMS (SUCH AS SECURITY, DISARMAMENT, AND BELLIGERENT WARLORDS), KARZAI PROMISED... "TO FACE THESE ISSUES AND BRING CONSTITUTIONAL REFORM AND DEMOCRATIC ELECTIONS IN THE UPCOMING YEAR."

ON DECEMBER 30, MITCH DANIELS, THE ADMINISTRATION'S DIRECTOR OF THE OFFICE OF MANAGEMENT AND BUDGET, ESTIMATES THAT A WAR WITH IRAQ WOULD COST FROM $50 BILLION TO $60 BILLION, SUBSTANTIALLY LESS THAN THE EARLIER ESTIMATE OF $100 BILLION TO $200 BILLION.

AS 2002 ENDED, THE U.S. ARMY SENT 15,000 COMBAT TROOPS FROM FT. STEWART, GA., TO KUWAIT, WHERE 4,000 WERE ALREADY IN TRAINING. THIS WAS THE LARGEST DEPLOYMENT TO THE AREA SINCE THE 1991 GULF WAR.

THOUGH UN INSPECTORS CENSURED IRAQ ON JANUARY 9, 2003, FOR NOT REVEALING ANY NEW DETAILS OF ITS CURRENT WEAPONS PROGRAM, THEY CONCEDED THAT NO REAL PROOF HAD BEEN DISCOVERED THAT ILLEGAL WEAPONS HAD BEEN HIDDEN.

ON JANUARY 10, DEFENSE SECRETARY RUMSFELD ISSUED AN ORDER ASSIGNING 35,000 ADDITIONAL TROOPS TO THE PERSIAN GULF REGION. THIS WAS PRESENTED AS APPLYING MORE PRESSURE ON SADDAM TO OBEY THE UN RESOLUTION TO DISARM.

ON JANUARY 16, UN WEAPONS INSPECTORS FOUND 11 EMPTY CHEMICAL WARHEADS AT A STORAGE SITE IN SOUTHERN IRAQ. THE IRAQI LIAISON TO THE INSPECTORS CLAIMED THEY HAD BEEN REPORTED IN IRAQ'S DECLARATION TO THE UN AND DATED BACK TO THE 1980S.

ONE DAY LATER, THE BUSH ADMINISTRATION AND THE WEAPONS INSPECTORS REACHED VERY DIFFERENT CONCLUSIONS. THE INSPECTORS BELIEVED THEIR SEARCH WAS PROVING FRUITFUL. DR. MOHAMED ELBARADEI, CHIEF WEAPONS INSPECTOR, ADDED THAT WAR IS...

...THE WORST SCENARIO. IF WE CAN AVOID THAT, EVEN SPENDING A FEW MORE MONTHS TO DO OUR JOB, THAT IS TIME WELL SPENT.

BUT BUSH'S PRESS SECRETARY ARI FLEISCHER SAID...

...THE PRESIDENT VIEWS THIS AS TROUBLING AND SERIOUS.

POSSESSION OF CHEMICAL WARHEADS IS NOT A GOOD INDICATION THAT [SADDAM] HAS DISARMED.

SENATOR EDWARD KENNEDY, SPEAKING ON JANUARY 21 AT THE NATIONAL PRESS CLUB, ACCUSED THE ADMINISTRATION OF TRYING TO GOAD AMERICA INTO WAR AT THE COST OF OUR ANTITERRORISM EFFORTS AND OUR DOMESTIC AGENDA. HE WENT ON TO SAY... "THIS IS THE WRONG WAR AT THE WRONG TIME."

BRAK-ATAK-TAK-

THE RELATIVE CALM OF THE AFGHAN WAR WAS BROKEN WHEN 350 AMERICAN AND ALLIED TROOPS FOUGHT THROUGH THE NIGHT AGAINST AN ARMY OF REBELS IN THE NATION'S SOUTHEAST MOUNTAIN REGION. THE WAR HAD QUIETED DOWN, BUT IT WAS STILL VERY MUCH ALIVE.

SECOND STATE OF THE UNION ADDRESS, ON JANUARY 28, HE CLAIMED THAT INTELLIGENCE REPORTS POINTED TO SADDAM HUSSEIN AS AN AID TO THE TERRORISTS, WHO COULD GIVE THEM WEAPONS OF MASS DESTRUCTION THAT ULTIMATELY MIGHT BE USED AGAINST THE UNITED STATES.

IMAGINE THOSE 19 HIJACKERS WITH OTHER WEAPONS AND OTHER PLANS, THIS TIME ARMED BY SADDAM HUSSEIN.

EVIDENCE FROM INTELLIGENCE SOURCES, SECRET COMMUNICATIONS, AND STATEMENTS BY PEOPLE NOW IN CUSTODY REVEAL THAT SADDAM HUSSEIN AIDS AND PROTECTS TERRORISTS, INCLUDING MEMBERS OF AL QAEDA.

DAYS LATER, CHIEF UN WEAPONS INSPECTOR HANS BLIX QUESTIONED THE PRESIDENT'S ASSERTIONS. BLIX SAID HE HAD SEEN NO PERSUASIVE PROOFS OF SADDAM'S SUPPOSED TIES TO AL QAEDA.

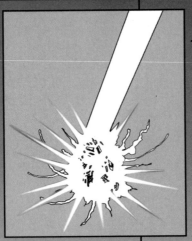

IN A *WASHINGTON POST*/ABC NEWS POLL, CONDUCTED IN EARLY FEBRUARY, HALF OF THOSE INTERVIEWED BELIEVED THAT WEAPONS INSPECTORS SHOULD BE GIVEN ONLY A FEW MORE WEEKS TO SEARCH FOR WEAPONS OF MASS DESTRUCTION BEFORE AMERICA GOES TO WAR.
IF THERE WAS A WAR...
19% BELIEVED THE WAR WOULD BE OVER IN A FEW WEEKS.
32% BELIEVED IT WOULD LAST FOR SEVERAL MONTHS.
45% BELIEVED IT WOULD CONTINUE FOR A YEAR OR MORE.

THE *COLUMBIA* SPACE SHUTTLE BROKE UP ON ITS ATTEMPTED REENTRY INTO EARTH'S ATMOSPHERE ON FEBRUARY 1, KILLING ALL SEVEN ASTRONAUTS ABOARD AND SCATTERING DEBRIS AND REMAINS OVER TEXAS AND LOUISIANA.

IT WOULD TAKE MONTHS FOR NASA TO LEARN THE CAUSE OF THE TRAGEDY. ONE MAJOR THEORY WAS THAT A PIECE OF INSULATION STRUCK PROTECTIVE TILES DURING ITS INITIAL TAKEOFF ON JANUARY 16, FROM CAPE CANAVERAL.

SECRETARY OF STATE COLIN POWELL CONTINUED TO PRESS THE AMERICAN CASE FOR WAR AGAINST IRAQ IN HIS ADDRESS TO THE UN SECURITY COUNCIL ON FEBRUARY 5. SHOWING SATELLITE PHOTOGRAPHS OF WHAT HE CLAIMED WERE CHEMICAL AND BIOLOGICAL FACILITIES IN IRAQ, HE SAID...

LEAVING SADDAM HUSSEIN IN POSSESSION OF WEAPONS OF MASS DESTRUCTION FOR A FEW MORE MONTHS OR YEARS IS NOT AN OPTION...

...NOT IN A POST-SEPTEMBER 11TH WORLD.

UNITED

IN A *NEW YORK TIMES*/CBS POLL IN MID-FEBRUARY, THE MAJORITY OF AMERICANS FAVORED GIVING MORE TIME TO UN WEAPONS INSPECTORS. THE PRESIDENT'S APPROVAL RATING WAS 54%, DOWN FROM 64% A MONTH BEFORE.

AMERICAN PRESSURE ON IRAQ CONTINUED THROUGH FEBRUARY AND EARLY MARCH...

DEFENSE SECRETARY RUMSFELD STATED THAT HE HAD...

...CONCERN ABOUT SADDAM HUSSEIN USING WEAPONS OF MASS DESTRUCTION AGAINST HIS OWN PEOPLE AND BLAMING US.

WHITE HOUSE PRESS SECRETARY ARI FLEISCHER SAID IRAQ MUST "COMPLETELY AND TOTALLY" DISARM OR ITS LEADERS MUST...

...GO INTO EXILE.

THE IRAQI ACTIONS ARE PROPAGANDA WRAPPED IN A LIE INSIDE A FALSEHOOD.

AND THE PRESIDENT SAID...

IF THE COUNCIL RESPONDS TO IRAQ'S DEFIANCE WITH MORE EXCUSES AND DELAYS, IF ALL ITS AUTHORITY PROVES TO BE EMPTY, THE UNITED NATIONS WILL BE SEVERELY WEAKENED AS A SOURCE OF STABILITY AND ORDER.

I WILL NOT LEAVE THE AMERICAN PEOPLE AT THE MERCY OF THE IRAQI DICTATOR AND HIS WEAPONS.

AND ALASKA SENATOR TED STEVENS WARNED...

WE HAVE RIGHT ON OUR SIDE AND WE HAVE MIGHT ON OUR SIDE AND SHOULD USE THAT MIGHT FOR THE BEST INTEREST OF THE WORLD IN THE FUTURE.

IN EARLY MARCH, DR. MOHAMED ELBARADEI, EXECUTIVE DIRECTOR OF THE INTERNATIONAL ATOMIC ENERGY AGENCY, BRANDED AS A FORGERY THE DOCUMENT PURPORTEDLY SHOWING THAT IRAQ BOUGHT URANIUM FROM NIGER. THIS DOCUMENT WAS USED BY THE PRESIDENT IN HIS STATE OF THE UNION ADDRESS AND BY SECRETARY POWELL IN HIS UN SPEECH AS PROOF OF HUSSEIN'S POSSESSION OF WEAPONS OF MASS DESTRUCTION.

IN A *NEW YORK TIMES/CBS* POLL ON MARCH 10, 58% OF AMERICANS NOW BELIEVE THE UN IS DOING A POOR JOB IN MANAGING THE IRAQ CRISIS; 55% OF AMERICANS WOULD BACK AN IRAQ INVASION WITHOUT UN APPROVAL AND 52% BELIEVE THE INSPECTORS SHOULD BE GIVEN MORE TIME.

FINALLY, ON MARCH 17, PRESIDENT BUSH GAVE SADDAM HUSSEIN 48 HOURS TO GO INTO EXILE OR FACE ATTACK FROM THE U.S. AND ITS ALLIES (WHICH MAINLY WERE THE BRITISH).

THE TYRANT WILL SOON BE GONE!

SADDAM HUSSEIN RESPONDED THE NEXT DAY, DESCRIBING THE PRESIDENT'S WARNING AS A...

...DESPICABLE AND RECKLESS ULTIMATUM.

AT 3:40 P.M. ON MARCH 19, PRESIDENT BUSH MET WITH VICE PRESIDENT CHENEY, DEFENSE SECRETARY RUMSFELD, NATIONAL SECURITY ADVISER RICE, AND CIA DIRECTOR GEORGE TENET. BY THAT EVENING, THE GROUP HAD DECIDED THAT INTELLIGENCE HAD GIVEN THEM "TARGETS OF OPPORTUNITY." THEY HAD LEARNED WHERE HUSSEIN AND SEVERAL OF HIS LEADERS WERE PURPORTED TO BE HIDING. THE PRESIDENT WAS REPORTED TO HAVE SAID...

...LET'S GO!

AT 10:15 THAT NIGHT, SPEAKING FROM THE OVAL OFFICE, PRESIDENT BUSH INFORMED THE NATION THAT WE WERE NOW AT WAR WITH IRAQ...

ON MY ORDERS, COALITION FORCES HAVE BEGUN STRIKING SELECTED TARGETS OF MILITARY IMPORTANCE...

THESE ARE OPENING STAGES IN WHAT WILL BE A BROAD AND CONCERTED CAMPAIGN.

HE ADDED, AND IT "COULD BE LONGER AND MORE DIFFICULT THAN SOME PREDICT."

EVEN BEFORE HE SPOKE, 2,000-POUND BOMBS AND TOMAHAWK CRUISE MISSILES--LAUNCHED FROM WARPLANES AND FROM U.S. SHIPS IN THE PERSIAN GULF--EXPLODED ON INSTALLATIONS NEAR BAGHDAD, WHERE HUSSEIN WAS BELIEVED TO BE... BUT WASN'T.

U.S. AND BRITISH WARPLANES ATTACKED IRAQI ARTILLERY POSITIONS IN SOUTHERN IRAQ TO PROTECT INVADING TROOPS. SPECIAL OPERATIONS FORCES WERE DROPPED BY PARACHUTE INTO DESERT REGIONS FROM U.S. PLANES AND HAD BEEN DROPPED BEFOREHAND INSIDE THE NATION.

BY THE NEXT DAY, AS MISSILES CONTINUED TO RAIN DOWN ON BAGHDAD, AMERICAN AND BRITISH TROOPS CROSSED THE DESERT FROM KUWAIT AND BEGAN THE GROUND CAMPAIGN.

45

MUCH OF THE WORLD REACTED ANGRILY.
RUSSIAN PRESIDENT VLADIMIR PUTIN CALLED
FOR AN IMMEDIATE HALT...

FRENCH PRESIDENT JACQUES CHIRAC
WARNED OF THE WAR'S CONSEQUENCES...

AND HUNDREDS OF THOUSANDS OF PEOPLE FROM ALL ACROSS THE WORLD PROTESTED THE INVASION.

IN THE FIRST DAYS, THE GOVERNMENT SEEMED READY TO COLLAPSE AS MORE THAN 1,300 BOMBS AND CRUISE MISSILES POUNDED THE COUNTRY, DEVASTATING BUILDINGS AND PALACES.

A *NEW YORK TIMES*/CBS POLL, ANNOUNCED ON MARCH 22, GAUGED THE PRESIDENT'S APPROVAL RATING AT 70%. HIS DISAPPROVAL RATING DROPPED TO 27%, 15% LOWER THAN BEFORE.

IN LESS THAN A WEEK, ALLIED FORCES HAD CROSSED MORE THAN 300 MILES THROUGH SOUTHERN IRAQ, PAUSING TO UNLEASH ARTILLERY FIRE AND HELICOPTERS NEAR BAGHDAD. ON MARCH 27, STANDING NEXT TO BRITISH PRIME MINISTER BLAIR AT CAMP DAVID, THE PRESIDENT DECLARED...

WE KNOW THE OUTCOME. IRAQ WILL BE DISARMED, THE IRAQI REGIME WILL BE ENDED, AND THE LONG-SUFFERING IRAQI PEOPLE WILL BE FREE.

HOWEVER, ON MARCH 29, AN OMINOUS NEW TACTIC WAS SEEN NEAR THE IRAQI CITY OF NAJAF. AN IRAQI SUICIDE BOMBER BLEW UP HIS TAXI AND KILLED FOUR U.S. SOLDIERS.

IRAQI VICE PRESIDENT TAHA YASSIN RAMADAN DECLARED THIS WAS ONLY THE BEGINNING. "ANY METHOD THAT STOPS OR KILLS THE ENEMY," HE SAID, "WILL BE USED."

ONE DAY LATER, IRAQI GENERAL HAZAM AL-RAWI CLAIMED THAT "4,000 VOLUNTEERS" FROM 23 DIFFERENT ARAB COUNTRIES WERE READY TO LAUNCH SUICIDE ATTACKS AGAINST AMERICAN FORCES.

HE ALSO LAUDED THE TAXI BOMBER, ADDING THAT HUSSEIN HAD AWARDED HIM TWO POSTHUMOUS MEDALS.

IN EARLY APRIL, 19-YEAR-OLD PFC JESSICA LYNCH WAS RESCUED BY SPECIAL FORCES FROM A HOSPITAL IN NASIRIYA WHERE SHE HAD BEEN HELD CAPTIVE SINCE MARCH 23.

SOME DAYS LATER, A FORCE OF 60 AMERICAN TANKS LED AN ARMORED BRIGADE INTO THE CENTER OF BAGHDAD, KILLING HUNDREDS OF IRAQI SOLDIERS. U.S. OFFICIALS CLAIMED THAT ONLY THREE OF THE SIX DEFENDING IRAQI DIVISONS REMAINED, AS WELL AS ONLY 92 OF IRAQ'S 2,500 TANKS.

I HEAR A LOT OF TALK HERE ABOUT HOW, YOU KNOW, WE'RE GOING TO IMPOSE THIS LEADER OR THAT LEADER.

FORGET IT! FROM DAY ONE WE HAVE SAID THE IRAQI PEOPLE ARE CAPABLE OF RUNNING THEIR OWN COUNTRY.

ON APRIL 9, AS IRAQIS STORMED THE STREETS IN THOUSANDS TOPPLING SADDAM'S STATUES AND LOOTING MINISTRIES AMERICAN LEADERS WERE ELATED. VICE PRESIDENT CHENEY AT THAT TIME LABELED SOME CRITICS OF THE WAR AS "RETIRED MILITARY OFFICERS EMBEDDED IN TV STUDIOS."

VIOLENCE AND UNCONTROLLABLE LOOTING CONTINUED IN BAGHDAD IN THE DAYS FOLLOWING, AS MUCH OF THE CITY HAD TO GO WITHOUT ESSENTIAL SERVICES OR PROTECTION.
THE NATIONAL MUSEUM OF IRAQ WAS STILL ANOTHER TRAGIC CASUALTY AS 170,000 ARTIFACTS WERE LOOTED DURING THE DAYS OF APRIL 10 AND APRIL 11.
STILL, ON APRIL 14, THE PENTAGON DECLARED THAT MAJOR COMBAT OPERATIONS IN IRAQ WERE OVER, AND PRESIDENT BUSH ONE DAY LATER SAID...

THE REGIME OF SADDAM HUSSEIN IS NO MORE.

AT THE SAME TIME, THOUSANDS OF SHIITE IRAQIS--THE MAJORITY OF MUSLIMS IN IRAQ, WHO HAD BEEN KEPT FROM POWER BY SADDAM HUSSEIN, A SUNNI--DEMONSTRATED IN NASIRIYA, CALLING FOR A MAJOR ROLE FOR THEIR LEADERS IN THE NEW GOVERNMENT.

IN MID-APRIL, BY VIRTUE OF A NEW FEDERAL TRANSPORTATION AGENCY PRECAUTION TAKEN SINCE THE 9/11 ATTACKS, 46 AIRLINE PILOTS, WHO HAD ALL JUST COMPLETED A REQUIRED TRAINING COURSE, ENTERED THEIR COMPANIES' COCKPITS EQUIPPED WITH .40-CALIBER SEMI-AUTOMATIC HANDGUNS.

DURING THAT TIME, THE BECHTEL GROUP WAS GIVEN THE FIRST IMPORTANT CONTRACT IN THE RECONSTRUCTION OF IRAQ. WORTH $680 MILLION, THE AWARD RILED SEVERAL EUROPEAN AND BRITISH COMPANIES THAT WERE NOT EVEN CONSIDERED.

IN AN INTERVIEW WITH NBC NEWS ON APRIL 24, PRESIDENT BUSH DECLARED THAT IRAQI SOURCES HAD INFORMED US THAT HUSSEIN MAY HAVE DESTROYED OR DISSEMINATED WEAPONS OF MASS DESTRUCTION BEFORE THE WAR. HE ADDED THAT THE WAR WAS MORE DIFFICULT THAN EXPECTED, AND WHEN ASKED IF IRAQI STABILITY COULD TAKE TWO YEARS TO ATTAIN, HE ANSWERED...

IT COULD, IT COULD. OR LESS. WHO KNOWS?

I THINK THERE'S GOING TO BE SKEPTICISM UNTIL PEOPLE FIND OUT THERE WAS IN FACT A WEAPONS OF MASS DESTRUCTION PROGRAM.

AND SO WE WILL FIND THEM.

BUT IT'S GOING TO TAKE TIME.

SEVERAL DAYS LATER, NIZAR HINDAWI, AN IMPORTANT IRAQI SCIENTIST, CLAIMED THAT THE SUPPOSED REVELATIONS MADE BY HIMSELF AND OTHER SCIENTISTS CONCERNING THE EXISTENCE OF AN IRAQI BIOLOGICAL WARFARE PROGRAM...

...WERE ALL LIES.

ON MAY 1, THE PRESIDENT, DRESSED IN A GREEN FLIGHT SUIT AND A WHITE HELMET, HELPED PILOT A NAVY JET THAT FLEW...

...TO THE DECK OF THE U.S. AIRCRAFT CARRIER ABRAHAM LINCOLN OUTSIDE SAN DIEGO HARBOR.

THERE HE ADDRESSED THOUSANDS OF SAILORS AND AVIATORS ABOARD THE SHIP AS WELL AS THE AMERICAN PUBLIC. JUST 43 DAYS SINCE HE HAD DECLARED THE START OF OPERATIONS AGAINST IRAQ, STANDING BENEATH A SIGN READING "MISSION ACCOMPLISHED," HE CLAIMED THE IRAQI BATTLE AS "ONE VICTORY IN A WAR ON TERROR THAT BEGAN ON SEPTEMBER 11, 2001, AND STILL GOES ON."

MISSION ACCOMPLISHED

HE ALSO DECLARED...

MAJOR COMBAT OPERATIONS IN IRAQ HAVE ENDED.

WE HAVE REMOVED AN ALLY OF AL QAEDA AND CUT OFF A SOURCE OF TERRORIST FUNDING.

NO TERRORIST NETWORK WILL GAIN WEAPONS OF MASS DESTRUCTION FROM THE IRAQI REGIME BECAUSE THAT REGIME IS NO MORE.

RETIRED DIPLOMAT L. PAUL BREMER III WAS NAMED BY THE PRESIDENT, IN EARLY MAY, AS HIS SPECIAL ENVOY TO IRAQ, REPLACING GEN. JAY GARNER.
BREMER WOULD NOW BE THE SENIOR CIVILIAN HEADING THE REBUILDING OF IRAQ'S GOVERNMENT AND ITS INFRASRUCTURE.

INSIDERS SUGGESTED THIS REPRESENTED THE PRESIDENT'S SHIFT FROM MILITARY OCCUPATION TO CIVILIAN ADMINISTRATION.

IN MID-MAY, FOUR SYNCHRONIZED TRUCK BOMBINGS IN RIYADH, SAUDI ARABIA, KILLED 20 PEOPLE, 7 OF WHOM WERE AMERICANS, ON THE EVE OF SECRETARY POWELL'S PLANNED VISIT.

POWELL DECLARED THAT THE BOMBINGS APPEAR TO BE THE WORK OF AL QAEDA.

IN AN APPARENT REVERSAL, THE U.S. AND BRITAIN POSTPONED PLANS TO HAVE IRAQIS FORM AN INTERIM GOVERNMENT BY THE END OF MAY. ALLIED OFFICIALS WILL STAY IN CONTROL INDEFINITELY, NEW CIVILIAN ADMINISTRATOR BREMER INDICATED TO EXILED IRAQI LEADERS.
IN LATE MAY, AT A SENATE FOREIGN RELATIONS COMMITTEE HEARING WITH DEPUTY DEFENSE SECRETARY WOLFOWITZ, DEMOCRATS AND SEVERAL REPUBLICANS CRITICIZED THE ADMINISTRATION'S IRAQI STRATEGY. "THE PLANNING FOR PEACE," COMMENTED REPUBLICAN LUGAR, "WAS MUCH LESS DEVELOPED THAN THE PLANNING FOR WAR." DEMOCRAT BIDEN ADDED...

WHEN IS THE PRESIDENT GOING TO TELL THE AMERICAN PEOPLE THAT WE'RE LIKELY TO BE IN THE COUNTRY FOR THREE, FOUR, FIVE, SIX, EIGHT, TEN YEARS?

IT IS POSSIBLE THINGS WILL GO FASTER.

51

NEAR THE END OF MAY, THE ADMINISTRATION CLAIMED IT WAS "HIGHLY CONFIDENT" THAT TWO STRANGE TRAILERS FOUND IN IRAQ RECENTLY WERE MOBILE UNITS THAT PRODUCED KILLER GERMS FOR HUSSEIN.
THESE WERE THE "STRONGEST EVIDENCE TO DATE," THEY SAID, "THAT IRAQ WAS HIDING A BIOLOGICAL WARFARE PROGRAM."
ONE WEEK LATER, HOWEVER, INTELLIGENCE ANALYSTS WHO HAD EXAMINED THE EVIDENCE DISPUTED THE CONCLUSIONS, THOUGH THE CIA STOOD BEHIND THEIR ASSERTIONS.

AMERICAN OFFICIALS RETREATED FROM AN EARLIER POLICY AND PERMITTED IRAQIS TO KEEP AK-47 ASSAULT RIFLES IN HOMES AND BUSINESSES.
THEY CONCEDED THAT DISARMING IRAQIS WAS DIFFICULT WHEN THEIR SECURITY WAS SO FRAGILE.

DURING THE FIRST WEEK OF JUNE, AFGHAN SOLDIERS KILLED 40 TALIBAN REBELS NEAR THREE SOUTHERN VILLAGES. THIS WAS A REMINDER OF THE GRAVE TALIBAN MENACE THAT STILL REMAINED IN AFGHANISTAN.

IT WAS DISCLOSED, IN EARLY JUNE, THAT TWO IMPORTANT AL QAEDA LEADERS IN U.S. CUSTODY HAD CLAIMED THEIR GROUP DID NOT WORK WITH HUSSEIN.
ABU ZUBAYDAH, CAPTURED IN MARCH 2002, HAD DECLARED THAT BIN LADEN HAD REJECTED THE IDEA.
IN A SEPARATE INTERVIEW, KHALID SHEIKH MOHAMMED, AL QAEDA'S OPERATIONS CHIEF, HAD AGREED THAT THEY DID NOT WORK WITH THE IRAQI CHIEF.

RETIRING UN CHIEF WEAPONS INSPECTOR HANS BLIX, IN A MID-JUNE INTERVIEW, WONDERED WHY THE AMERICAN-BRITISH ALLIES BELIEVED THEY'D FIND STOCKPILES OF ILLEGAL WEAPONS WHEN UN INVESTIGATORS HADN'T.

IS THE UNITED NATIONS ON A DIFFERENT PLANET? ARE REPORTS FROM HERE TOTALLY UNREAD SOUTH OF THE HUDSON?

BARELY TWO MONTHS SINCE AMERICAN AND BRITISH TROOPS WERE GREETED JOYOUSLY AS EMANCIPATORS, BY THE END OF JUNE THEY WERE BEING CRITICIZED FOR ALL THAT HAD GONE WRONG.

BUT MANY OF THE PROBLEMS WERE THE RESULT OF SABOTAGE AND LOOTING BY IRAQIS THEMSELVES.

TRUCK DRIVER LYMAN FARIS, A NATURALIZED CITIZEN FROM KASHMIR, PLEADED GUILTY TO GIVING SUPPORT TO THE TERRORISTS AND FACES 20 YEARS IN PRISON. HE WAS ORIGINALLY ARRESTED IN MARCH.

ON JULY 6, AN OP-ED ARTICLE IN *THE NEW YORK TIMES* BY FORMER AMBASSADOR JOSEPH C. WILSON APPEARED AND IGNITED A HUGE CONTROVERSY. WILSON, WHO HAD BEEN SENT TO NIGER TO INVESTIGATE THE SUPPOSED ATTEMPT BY HUSSEIN TO BUY URANIUM THERE, CLAIMED THE PRESIDENT HAD RELIED ON ERRONEOUS INFORMATION FOR HIS STATE OF THE UNION ACCUSATION.

IN LATE JUNE, AN AL QAEDA PLOT TO DESTROY THE BROOKLYN BRIDGE AND OTHER TARGETS THE PREVIOUS MONTH WAS DISCLOSED BY FEDERAL OFFICIALS.

"BASED ON MY EXPERIENCE WITH THE ADMINISTRATION IN THE MONTHS LEADING UP TO THE WAR, I HAVE LITTLE CHOICE BUT TO CONCLUDE THAT SOME OF THE INTELLIGENCE RELATED TO IRAQ'S NUCLEAR PROGRAM WAS TWISTED TO EXAGGERATE THE IRAQI THREAT..."
ONE DAY LATER, THE ADMINISTRATION ADMITTED FOR THE FIRST TIME THAT THE INFORMATION MAY HAVE BEEN FLAWED.

THE FEDERAL BIPARTISAN COMMISSION FORMED TO INVESTIGATE THE 9/11 ATTACKS CRITICIZED FEDERAL AGENCIES, IN EARLY JULY, FOR HAMPERING THEIR INVESTIGATION.

CHAIR THOMAS KEAN AND VICE CHAIR LEE HAMILTON POINTED FINGERS AT THE DEFENSE AND JUSTICE DEPARTMENTS FOR NOT ANSWERING THEIR CALLS FOR DOCUMENTS AND TESTIMONY.

"THE PRESIDENT IS COMMITTED TO INSURING THAT THE COMMISSION HAS ALL THE INFORMATION IT NEEDS," SAID A WHITE HOUSE SPOKESPERSON.

AT MUCH THE SAME TIME, GEN. TOMMY FRANKS DECLARED THAT THE VIOLENCE IN IRAQ MADE A REDUCTION OF TROOPS UNLIKELY...

...FOR THE FORSEEABLE FUTURE.

MEANWHILE, SECRETARY RUMSFELD'S ESTIMATE OF MONTHLY WAR COSTS JUMPED FROM $2 BILLION PER MONTH TO $3.9 BILLION.

STANDING SHOULDER TO SHOULDER WITH PRESIDENT BUSH IN MID-JULY, PRIME MINISTER TONY BLAIR DECLARED THAT EVEN IF WEAPONS OF MASS DESTRUCTION WERE NOT FOUND, THE IRAQI CONFLICT WAS JUSTIFIED.

RESPONDING TO A TIP FROM AN IRAQI, AMERICAN FORCES SURROUNDED A HOUSE IN MOSUL IN LATE JULY, AND DEMANDED THE SURRENDER OF HUSSEIN'S SONS, UDAY AND QUSAY, WHO WERE INSIDE.

WHEN THEY REFUSED, A FIERCE SHOOTOUT TOOK PLACE THAT RESULTED IN THE DEATHS OF BOTH MEN.

A SCATHING 900-PAGE REPORT BY A JOINT PANEL OF HOUSE AND SENATE INTELLIGENCE COMMITTEES IN LATE JULY CRITICIZED THE CIA AND THE FBI FOR THEIR LACK OF UNDERSTANDING OF THE TERRORIST THREAT BEFORE 9/11 AND FOR MISSING CHANCES TO FOIL IT. FLORIDA SENATOR BOB GRAHAM, COCHAIRMAN OF THE INQUIRY, SAID...

THE ATTACKS OF SEPTEMBER 11 COULD HAVE BEEN PREVENTED IF THE RIGHT COMBINATION OF SKILL, COOPERATION, AND SOME GOOD LUCK HAD BEEN BROUGHT TO TASK.

SEVERAL DAYS LATER, THE PRESIDENT REFUSED TO DECLASSIFY A 28-PAGE SEGMENT OF THE REPORT CONCERNING THE SAUDI ROLE IN FINANCING...

...TERRORISTS. HE CLAIMED IT WOULD...

...HELP THE ENEMY.

SOON AFTER, IN HIS FIRST NEWS CONFERENCE IN FIVE MONTHS, MR. BUSH DENIED HAVING EXAGGERATED THE NEED TO GO TO WAR AND SAID THAT FORCES ARE "ON THE HUNT" TO GET HUSSEIN.

A CAR BOMB BLEW UP NEAR THE JORDANIAN EMBASSY IN BAGHDAD ON AUGUST 7, KILLING 11 AND WOUNDING 65 PEOPLE. THIS WAS THE WAR'S BLOODIEST DAY IN THREE MONTHS.

WITH THE NAMING OF HIS WIFE, VALERIE PLAME, AS A CIA COVERT OPERATOR IN EARLY AUGUST, FORMER AMBASSADOR JOSEPH WILSON CLAIMED HE HAD BECOME AN ADMINISTRATION TARGET BECAUSE OF HIS OP-ED PIECE IN THE NEW YORK TIMES.

THE DISCLOSURE OF MS. PLAME'S NAME WAS MADE BY COLUMNIST ROBERT NOVAK, WHO GAVE A SENIOR ADMINISTRATION OFFICIAL AS HIS SOURCE.

SPEAKING FROM HIS HOME IN TEXAS ON AUGUST 8, WITH VICE PRESIDENT CHENEY AND SECRETARY RUMSFELD AT HIS SIDE, PRESIDENT BUSH SAID...

I AM PLEASED WITH THE PROGRESS WE'VE MADE [IN IRAQ] BUT FULLY RECOGNIZE WE'VE GOT A LOT OF WORK TO DO.

THE MOST TRAGIC DAY IN AFGHANISTAN IN ALMOST A YEAR OCCURRED WHEN 55 PEOPLE WERE KILLED IN TWO VIOLENT ACTIONS THERE IN MID-AUGUST.

FIFTEEN DIED WHEN A BOMB BLEW UP A BUS IN HELMAND PROVINCE, AND 40 GOVERNMENT SOLDIERS WERE KILLED BY TALIBAN GUERRILLAS IN KHOST, CLOSE TO THE PAKISTANI BORDER.

DAYS LATER, A CEMENT MIXER LOADED WITH EXPLOSIVES WAS DRIVEN INTO THE SIDE OF THE UN COMPOUND IN BAGHDAD.

SEVENTEEN PEOPLE WERE KILLED, MORE THAN 100 WERE WOUNDED, AND THE COMPOUND ITSELF WAS DEVASTATED.

A HORRENDOUS END TO THIS BLOODY MONTH TOOK PLACE IN NAJAF, IRAQ, WHEN A POTENT CAR BOMB EXPLODED OUTSIDE THE SHIITE MOSQUE OF IMAM ALI ON AUGUST 29, KILLING ALMOST 100 PEOPLE GATHERED THERE.

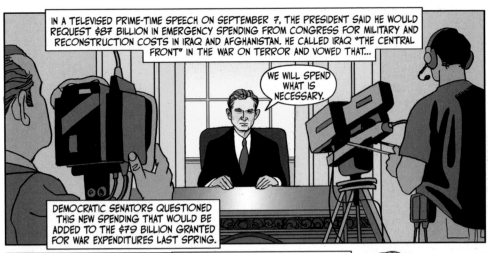

IN A TELEVISED PRIME-TIME SPEECH ON SEPTEMBER 7, THE PRESIDENT SAID HE WOULD REQUEST $87 BILLION IN EMERGENCY SPENDING FROM CONGRESS FOR MILITARY AND RECONSTRUCTION COSTS IN IRAQ AND AFGHANISTAN. HE CALLED IRAQ "THE CENTRAL FRONT" IN THE WAR ON TERROR AND VOWED THAT...

WE WILL SPEND WHAT IS NECESSARY.

DEMOCRATIC SENATORS QUESTIONED THIS NEW SPENDING THAT WOULD BE ADDED TO THE $79 BILLION GRANTED FOR WAR EXPENDITURES LAST SPRING.

ON SEPTEMBER 11, 2003, THE SECOND ANNIVERSARY OF THE TERRORIST ATTACKS, AN ANALYSIS BY NEW YORK TIMES CORRESPONDENTS DECLARED THAT WORLD OPINION HAD GONE FROM "POST-9/11 SYMPATHY" TO "POST-IRAQ ANTIPATHY."

American Embassy

NO IRAQ WAR

NO

SAY NO

STOP BOMBING CHILDREN

ONE WEEK LATER, DEPARTMENT OF DEFENSE OFFICIALS IDENTIFIED AMERICA'S MOST POTENT FOE IN IRAQ AS IRAQI RESENTMENT TO MILITARY OCCUPATION.

IN MID-SEPTEMBER, THE PRESIDENT CALLED FOR AN EXPANSION OF ENFORCEMENT POWERS IN THE PATRIOT ACT IN A SPEECH AT THE FBI TRAINING ACADEMY IN QUANTICO. DECLARING THAT THERE WERE "UNREASONABLE OBSTACLES" IN THIS FIGHT AGAINST TERRORISTS, HE SAID, "IF WE CAN USE THESE SUBPOENAS TO CATCH CROOKED DOCTORS, THE CONGRESS SHOULD ALLOW LAW ENFORCEMENT OFFICIALS TO USE THEM IN CATCHING TERRORISTS."

IT WAS REVEALED ON SEPTEMBER 17 THAT THE U.S. NOW PLANNED FOR A 40,000-TROOP IRAQI ARMY TO BE IN THE FIELD BY NEXT YEAR.

THIS NEW TIMETABLE, GREATLY ACCELERATING EARLIER PLANS, RELIED ON USING OFFICERS FROM HUSSEIN'S ARMY AS BOOT CAMP AIDES.

ADAMANTLY DEFENDING THE IRAQ WAR TO THE UN GENERAL ASSEMBLY ON SEPTEMBER 26, PRESIDENT BUSH REJECTED FRENCH AND GERMAN REQUESTS FOR A TRANSFER OF POWER TO THE IRAQI GOVERNING COUNCIL.

SELF-GOVERNMENT, HE DECLARED, MUST BE AN "ORDERLY" PROCESS THAT SHOULD BE "NEITHER HURRIED NOR DELAYED." HE ADDED...

IRAQ'S FORMER DICTATOR WILL NEVER AGAIN USE WEAPONS OF MASS DESTRUCTION.

FRENCH PRESIDENT JACQUES CHIRAC COUNTERED...

IN AN OPEN WORLD, NO ONE CAN LIVE IN ISOLATION, NO ONE CAN ACT ALONE IN THE NAME OF ALL, AND NO ONE CAN ACCEPT THE ANARCHY OF A SOCIETY WITHOUT RULES.

ON SEPTEMBER 25, UN SECRETARY-GENERAL KOFI ANNAN DECLARED HE WOULD REMOVE MOST OF THE UN'S 86 STAFF MEMBERS IN IRAQ BECAUSE OF SECURITY CONCERNS.

A CNN/USA TODAY/GALLUP POLL FINDS THE PRESIDENT'S APPROVAL RATING AT 50%, THE LOWEST SINCE HE TOOK OFFICE.

DAVID KAY, AMERICA'S CHIEF WEAPONS INSPECTOR IN IRAQ, INFORMED CONGRESS ON OCTOBER 2 THAT AFTER ITS THREE-MONTH SEARCH, HIS GROUP HAD DISCOVERED NO ILLEGAL WEAPONS. HE LABELED THIS AN "INTERIM PROGRESS REPORT" AND EXPECTED TO BE SEARCHING FOR ANOTHER SIX TO NINE MONTHS.

THE NEXT DAY, THE PRESIDENT DECLARED THAT KAY'S REPORT PROVED THAT "WE DID THE RIGHT THING" IN INVADING IRAQ. HE ADDED... "SADDAM HUSSEIN WAS A DANGER TO THE WORLD." HOUSE MINORITY LEADER DEMOCRAT NANCY PELOSI COUNTERED:

IT WAS CLEAR TO ME THAT THERE WAS NO IMMINENCE OF A THREAT FROM WEAPONS OF MASS DESTRUCTION.

IN EARLY OCTOBER, ALMOST 700 NEW IRAQI SOLDIERS FINISHED BASIC TRAINING, FORMING THE FIRST IRAQI BATTALION EXPECTED TO FIGHT ALONGSIDE U.S. TROOPS.

BLAM! BLAM! BLAM!

ON OCTOBER 9, TWO U.S. SOLDIERS AND TWO IRAQIS WERE KILLED BY FOLLOWERS OF SHIITE LEADER MUQTADA AL-SADR IN THE IMPOVERISHED BAGHDAD DISTRICT OF SADR CITY, NAMED FOR AL-SADR'S FATHER.

THIS MARKED THE FIRST TIME THAT AMERICAN FORCES HAD BEEN TARGETED BY IRAQIS OTHER THAN FOLLOWERS OF SADDAM HUSSEIN, WHO ARE MAINLY SUNNI.

ONE DAY LATER, A CROWD OF ALMOST 10,000, WHO BLAMED AMERICA FOR THE DEATH OF TWO IRAQIS, GATHERED IN SADR CITY TO DEMONSTRATE.

SHEIKH ABDEL HADI AL-DARAJI, AN ASSOCIATE OF SADR'S, DECLARED THAT NO AMERICAN SHOULD BE ALLOWED IN SADR CITY.

AMERICA, HE SAID, "IS NOTHING BUT A BIG TERRORIST ORGANIZATION."

VROOM!

VIOLENCE CONTINUED. SOON AFTERWARD, A LARGE CAR BOMB BLEW UP IN FRONT OF A BAGHDAD HOTEL KILLING SIX IRAQI SECURITY GUARDS AND WOUNDING DOZENS OF CIVILIANS.

THE HOTEL WAS KNOWN FOR BEING USED BY IRAQI GOVERNMENT COUNCIL MEMBERS AND AMERICANS.

BOTH THEATERS OF WAR WERE HEATING UP.

NEAR THE SAME TIME, TALIBAN FIGHTERS ATTACKED A GOVERNMENT OFFICE IN THE AFGHAN PROVINCE OF ZABUL, KILLING SEVEN AND WOUNDING TWO.

THE UN SECURITY COUNCIL, ON OCTOBER 16, UNANIMOUSLY PASSED A JOINT AMERICAN-BRITISH RESOLUTION AUTHORIZING AN INTERNATIONAL FORCE UNDER U.S. COMMAND IN IRAQ.

ALSO STATED IN THE RESOLUTION WAS A DECEMBER 15 DEADLINE FOR THE IRAQI GOVERNING COUNCIL TO FORM A PLAN AND A SCHEDULE FOR ADOPTING A CONSTITUTION.

THIS RESOLUTION WILL HELP MARSHAL EVEN MORE INTERNATIONAL SUPPORT FOR A NEW, DEMOCRATIC IRAQ.

SAID PRESIDENT BUSH, WHO CONSIDERED THE RESOLUTION AN IMPORTANT TRIUMPH.

IN OCTOBER, THREE U.S. SERVICEMEN IN A PATROL OF TEN WERE KILLED OUTSIDE KARBALA BY THE HEAVILY ARMED GUARDS OF IRAQI SHIITE CLERIC MAHMOUD AL-HASSANI. THE CLERIC WAS A KNOWN ALLY OF ANTI-AMERICAN IRAQI LEADER MUQTADA AL-SADR.

BY OCTOBER 18, 101 AMERICAN SERVICEMEN HAD DIED IN IRAQ SINCE PRESIDENT BUSH DECLARED THE END OF HOSTILITIES ON MAY 1.

WHUMF!

IN LATE OCTOBER, A COORDINATED ASSAULT OF SUICIDE BOMBERS IN BAGHDAD KILLED 34 PEOPLE AND WOUNDED MORE THAN 200.

SUCCESSFULLY TARGETED WERE THE RED CROSS HEADQUARTERS AND FOUR IRAQI POLICE STATIONS, WHILE A SIXTH ATTEMPT WAS STOPPED.

OCCURRING ON THE FIRST DAY OF RAMADAN, THE MONTHLONG MUSLIM OBSERVANCE OF DAYTIME FASTING, THESE VIOLENT ATTACKS OPENED A NEW CHAPTER IN THE ANTI-AMERICAN INSURGENCY.

IN EARLY NOVEMBER, 16 AMERICAN SOLDIERS WERE KILLED AND 20 WERE WOUNDED WHEN IRAQI INSURGENTS SHOT DOWN A U.S. HELICOPTER NEAR FALLUJAH. THIS WAS THE DEADLIEST ASSAULT ON AMERICAN FORCES SINCE THE INVASION OF IRAQ.

ON NOVEMBER 3, THE SENATE APPROVED THE ADMINISTRATION'S REQUEST FOR AN ADDITIONAL $87.5 BILLION FOR OCCUPYING AND REBUILDING IRAQ AND AFGHANISTAN.

LATER THAT MONTH, AFTER PROTESTS FROM IRAQIS, AND ESPECIALLY IRAQI KURDS, TURKEY WITHDREW ITS OFFER OF CONTRIBUTING 10,000 TROOPS TO COALITION FORCES IN IRAQ. KURDS AND OTHER IRAQIS HAD BEEN ANGERED THAT HELP MIGHT COME FROM THIS NATION UNDER WHOSE RULE THEY ONCE HAD GREATLY SUFFERED.

HOOSH!

THERE WERE THEN 24,000 NON-AMERICAN TROOPS STATIONED IN IRAQ, HALF OF WHOM WERE BRITISH.

ON NOVEMBER 12, IN A DEADLY ATTACK ON ITALIAN COALITION FORCES IN IRAQ, A CAR BOMB EXPLODED OUTSIDE THEIR HEADQUARTERS IN NASIRIYA, KILLING 17 ITALIANS AND 9 IRAQIS AND WOUNDING 105 OTHERS.

ITALY'S PRIME MINISTER, SILVIO BERLUSCONI, DECLARED THAT HIS NATION REMAINED COMMITTED TO THE U.S.-LED STRATEGY IN IRAQ.

ON NOVEMBER 12, THE DATE FOR ESTABLISHING A TEMPORARY SELF-GOVERNMENT IN IRAQ WAS MOVED UP AT AMERICA'S URGING, PARTLY IN RESPONSE TO THE INCREASED ATTACKS ON COALITION FORCES. ELECTIONS WERE NOW SCHEDULED FOR THE FIRST HALF OF 2004. ALSO DEBATED WAS THE POSSIBILITY OF DECREASING AMERICAN FORCES BY THE FOLLOWING NOVEMBER. AN UNNAMED OFFICIAL DECLARED...

WHATEVER WE WANT TO CALL OURSELVES, WE ARE AN OCCUPYING POWER...

...AND WE JUST CANNOT STAY IN POWER THAT LONG.

KRASH!

IN MID-NOVEMBER, TWO BLACK HAWK HELICOPTERS COLLIDED IN MIDAIR OVER MOSUL AS ONE SOARED UPWARD TO AVOID GROUND FIRE AND CRASHED INTO THE OTHER. SEVENTEEN SOLDIERS WERE KILLED AND FIVE WERE WOUNDED.

ON NOVEMBER 20, WHILE PRESIDENT BUSH WAS MEETING WITH PRIME MINISTER TONY BLAIR IN LONDON, TERRORISTS EXPLODED TWO TRUCK BOMBS AT TWO BRITISH SITES IN ISTANBUL, TURKEY, KILLING MORE THAN 27 PEOPLE AND WOUNDING 450.

AL QAEDA AND THE TURKISH TERRORIST GROUP IBDA-C CLAIMED RESPONSIBILITY.

ON NOVEMBER 26, IRAQ'S MOST INFLUENTIAL CLERIC, SHIITE GRAND AYATOLLAH ALI AL-SISTANI, OPPOSED THE U.S. PROPOSAL FOR INDIRECT ELECTIONS, SEEMINGLY CHALLENGING AMERICAN PLANS. HIS AIDE, ABDUL AZIZ AL-HAKIM, DECLARED, "THE PEOPLE SHOULD HAVE A BASIC ROLE IN ISSUES CONCERNING THE DESTINY OF THEIR COUNTRY."

AT THE SAME TIME, AHMAD CHALABI, ONCE AN AMERICAN FAVORITE AND LATER A PART OF IRAQ'S INTERIM GOVERNING COUNCIL, SAID...

THE WHOLE THING WAS SET UP SO PRESIDENT BUSH COULD COME TO THE AIRPORT IN OCTOBER TO CONGRATULATE THE NEW IRAQI GOVERNMENT.

THIS WOULD BE ONE MONTH BEFORE THE AMERICAN ELECTIONS.

BACKGROUND

DURING THE REGIME OF SADDAM HUSSEIN, A MEMBER OF IRAQ'S SUNNI MINORITY, IRAQ'S GOVERNMENT WAS PURPORTEDLY NONSECTARIAN, THOUGH MOST OF THE KEY GOVERNMENT POSITIONS WERE HELD BY SUNNIS.

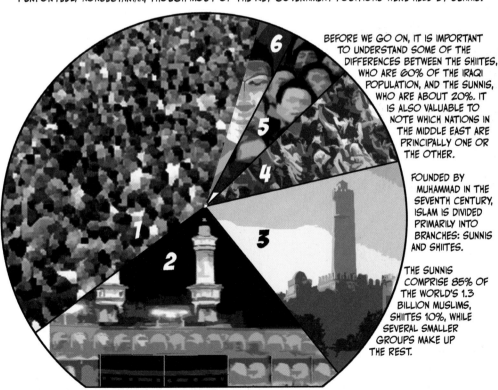

BEFORE WE GO ON, IT IS IMPORTANT TO UNDERSTAND SOME OF THE DIFFERENCES BETWEEN THE SHIITES, WHO ARE 60% OF THE IRAQI POPULATION, AND THE SUNNIS, WHO ARE ABOUT 20%. IT IS ALSO VALUABLE TO NOTE WHICH NATIONS IN THE MIDDLE EAST ARE PRINCIPALLY ONE OR THE OTHER.

FOUNDED BY MUHAMMAD IN THE SEVENTH CENTURY, ISLAM IS DIVIDED PRIMARILY INTO BRANCHES: SUNNIS AND SHIITES.

THE SUNNIS COMPRISE 85% OF THE WORLD'S 1.3 BILLION MUSLIMS, SHIITES 10%, WHILE SEVERAL SMALLER GROUPS MAKE UP THE REST.

THE WORLD'S MAJOR RELIGIONS

1. CHRISTIANITY: 2.1 BILLION. 2. ISLAM: 1.3 BILLION, INCLUDING 1 BILLION SUNNIS, 125 MILLION SHIITES. 3. NONRELIGIOUS: 1.1 BILLION. 4. HINDUISM: 900 MILLION. 5. CHINESE TRADITIONAL: 394 MILLION. 6. BUDDHISM: 376 MILLION.

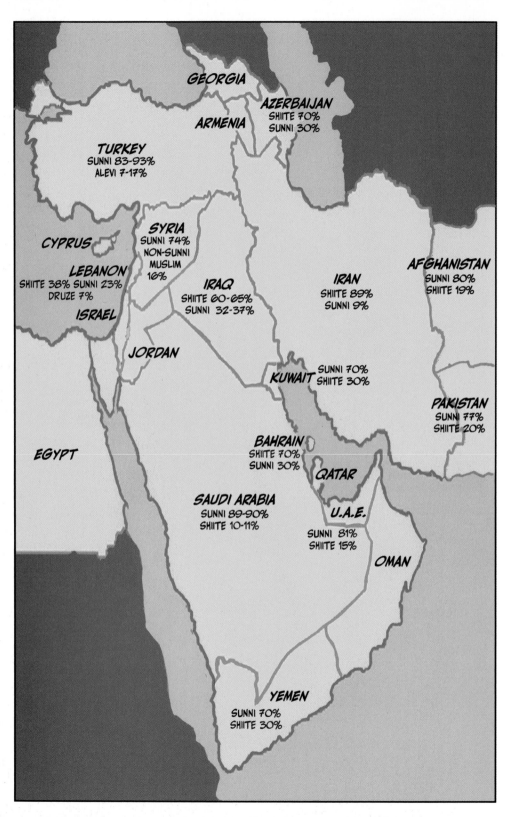

CHAPTER 6: INSURGENCY OR CIVIL WAR?

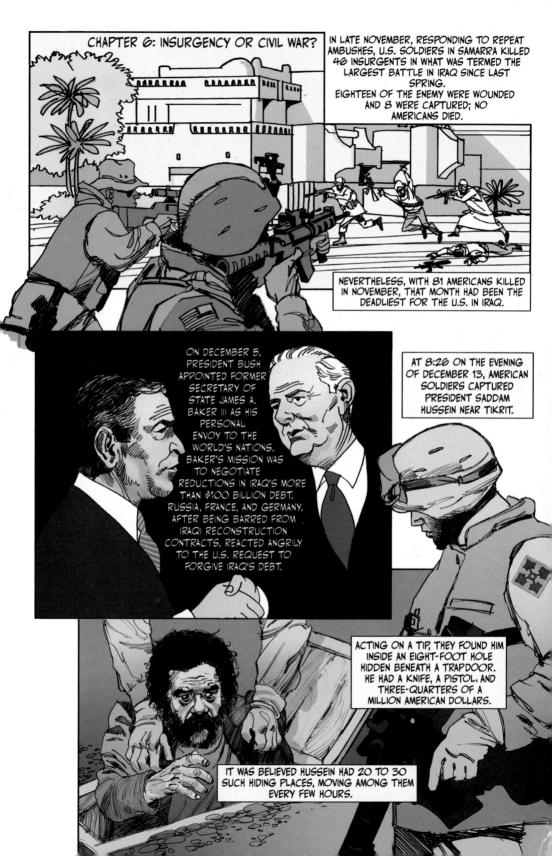

IN LATE NOVEMBER, RESPONDING TO REPEAT AMBUSHES, U.S. SOLDIERS IN SAMARRA KILLED 46 INSURGENTS IN WHAT WAS TERMED THE LARGEST BATTLE IN IRAQ SINCE LAST SPRING. EIGHTEEN OF THE ENEMY WERE WOUNDED AND 8 WERE CAPTURED; NO AMERICANS DIED.

NEVERTHELESS, WITH 81 AMERICANS KILLED IN NOVEMBER, THAT MONTH HAD BEEN THE DEADLIEST FOR THE U.S. IN IRAQ.

ON DECEMBER 5, PRESIDENT BUSH APPOINTED FORMER SECRETARY OF STATE JAMES A. BAKER III AS HIS PERSONAL ENVOY TO THE WORLD'S NATIONS. BAKER'S MISSION WAS TO NEGOTIATE REDUCTIONS IN IRAQ'S MORE THAN $100 BILLION DEBT. RUSSIA, FRANCE, AND GERMANY, AFTER BEING BARRED FROM IRAQI RECONSTRUCTION CONTRACTS, REACTED ANGRILY TO THE U.S. REQUEST TO FORGIVE IRAQ'S DEBT.

AT 8:26 ON THE EVENING OF DECEMBER 13, AMERICAN SOLDIERS CAPTURED PRESIDENT SADDAM HUSSEIN NEAR TIKRIT.

ACTING ON A TIP, THEY FOUND HIM INSIDE AN EIGHT-FOOT HOLE HIDDEN BENEATH A TRAPDOOR. HE HAD A KNIFE, A PISTOL, AND THREE-QUARTERS OF A MILLION AMERICAN DOLLARS.

IT WAS BELIEVED HUSSEIN HAD 20 TO 30 SUCH HIDING PLACES, MOVING AMONG THEM EVERY FEW HOURS.

COMMENTING ON THE CAPTURE OF HUSSEIN, PRESIDENT BUSH SAID...

GOOD RIDDANCE! THE WORLD IS BETTER OFF WITHOUT YOU.

THE PRESIDENT CHARACTERIZED SNARING THE IRAQI DESPOT AS THE CROWNING ACHIEVEMENT OF "AN EXTRAORDINARY YEAR FOR OUR COUNTRY." THEN HE ADDED THAT HE "WOULD ABSOLUTELY SEEK THE OFFICE [OF THE PRESIDENCY] AGAIN."

HUSSEIN'S CAPTURE DID NOT, HOWEVER, QUIET THE INSURGENCY. ON NOVEMBER 16, TWO CAR BOMBS WERE DETONATED AT POLICE STATIONS IN BAGHDAD, KILLING 6 IRAQI OFFICERS AND WOUNDING 20 OTHERS...

...FOLLOWED ONE DAY LATER BY A TRUCK BOMB IN BAGHDAD THAT KILLED 17 PEOPLE ON A BUS.

BY MID-DECEMBER, PRESIDENTIAL ENVOY JAMES BAKER LEARNED THAT BOTH FRANCE AND GERMANY HAD AGREED TO AID THE U.S. BY REDUCING IRAQ'S DEBTS.

VIOLENT ATTACKS CONTINUED DURING THE LAST DAYS OF 2003: 4 U.S. SOLDIERS WERE KILLED IN CENTRAL IRAQ AND 4 COALITION SOLDIERS AND 9 IRAQIS DIED IN KARBALA.

MORE THAN 100 IRAQI CIVILIANS WERE WOUNDED IN THESE ASSAULTS, WHICH OCCURRED LITTLE MORE THAN TWO WEEKS AFTER HUSSEIN'S CAPTURE.

AS THE NEW YEAR BEGAN, 2,000 AMERICAN SOLDIERS CONCLUDED A MONTHLONG SWEEP OF AFGHANISTAN'S SOUTHERN AND EASTERN REGIONS. MORE THAN 100 OF THE ENEMY WERE ARRESTED, AND 10 SUSPECTED TALIBAN OR AL QAEDA MEMBERS WERE KILLED IN THE OPERATION.

ON JANUARY 1, PAKISTAN'S GEN. PERVEZ MUSHARRAF RECEIVED A VOTE OF CONFIDENCE FROM PAKISTAN'S ELECTORAL COLLEGE TO LEGALLY STAY ON AS PRESIDENT.

HE HAD ORIGINALLY ASSUMED POWER THROUGH A BLOODLESS COUP IN 1999.

ON JANUARY 4, AFTER THREE WEEKS OF INTENSE DEBATE, AFGHANISTAN'S NEW CONSTITUTION WAS APPROVED BY 502 DELEGATES, CREATING A DEMOCRATIC SYSTEM OF TWO LEGISLATIVE HOUSES AND A DIRECTLY ELECTED PRESIDENCY. THE COUNTRY WAS RENAMED THE ISLAMIC REPUBLIC OF AFGHANISTAN.

ON JANUARY 8, SECRETARY OF STATE COLIN POWELL STATED THAT HE HAD SEEN NO EVIDENCE OF A LINK BETWEEN THE GOVERNMENT OF SADDAM HUSSEIN AND AL QAEDA.

I HAVE NOT SEEN SMOKING-GUN, CONCRETE EVIDENCE ABOUT THE CONNECTION.

BUT I THINK THE POSSIBILITY OF SUCH CONNECTIONS DID EXIST AND IT WAS PRUDENT TO CONSIDER THEM AT THE TIME THAT WE DID.

FOUR DAYS LATER, PAUL O'NEILL, THE PRESIDENT'S FIRST SECRETARY OF THE TREASURY, TOLD CBS'S *60 MINUTES* THAT PRESIDENT BUSH HAD FOCUSED ON OVERTHROWING HUSSEIN MONTHS BEFORE 9/11. HE DECLARED: "FROM THE VERY BEGINNING THERE WAS A CONVICTION THAT SADDAM HUSSEIN WAS A BAD GUY AND THAT HE NEEDED TO GO."

IN AN INTERVIEW WITH *TIME* MAGAZINE, O'NEILL ALSO CONCEDED THAT HE "NEVER SAW ANYTHING" THAT WAS EVIDENCE THAT IRAQ POSSESSED WEAPONS OF MASS DESTRUCTION.

ON JANUARY 18, A HUGE TRUCK BOMB BLEW UP AT THE MAIN GATE OF U.S. HEADQUARTERS IN BAGHDAD, KILLING 20 PEOPLE AND WOUNDING 60 MORE. THIS WAS THE DEADLIEST SUICIDE BOMBING IN IRAQ SINCE THE PREVIOUS AUGUST.

IN LATE JANUARY, THOMAS KEANE, CHAIR OF THE 9/11 COMMISSION, SOUGHT MORE TIME TO COMPLETE THE GROUP'S INVESTIGATION. THE FORMER NEW JERSEY GOVERNOR ASKED THAT THEIR DEADLINE OF MAY 2 BE EXTENDED TO AT LEAST JULY.

WE ARE TELLING THE CONGRESS AND THE PRESIDENT WHAT WE NEED IN ORDER TO DO THE BEST POSSIBLE JOB.

THE COMMISSION CITED THE ADMINISTRATION'S DELAY IN TURNING OVER PAPERS AS ONE REASON FOR THEIR REQUEST.

ON FEBRUARY 1, TWO SUICIDE BOMBERS, ACTING TEN MINUTES APART, BLEW UP TWO DIFFERENT KURDISH POLITICAL HEADQUARTERS IN KURDISH-CONTROLLED IRAQ, A REGION THAT HAD BEEN ENJOYING RELATIVE CALM.

THE TWO ATTACKS RESULTED IN 56 DEATHS AND WOUNDED MORE THAN 200 KURDS.

SIXTY U.S.-OPERATING LOCATIONS WERE REDUCED TO 26, WHICH WERE EXPECTED TO DROP TO 8 BY MID-APRIL.

IN EARLY FEBRUARY, BRIG. GEN. MARTIN E. DEMPSEY, RESPONSIBLE FOR BAGHDAD SECURITY, ORDERED A SHARP DROP IN AMERICAN TROOPS POLICING THE CITY. THE GENERAL DECLARED THE NEW IRAQI TROOPS "CAPABLE OF HANDLING THE THREAT."

ON FEBRUARY 4, APPEARING BEFORE BOTH HOUSE AND SENATE ARMED SERVICES COMMITTEES, SECRETARY OF DEFENSE RUMSFELD DEFENDED PREWAR INTELLIGENCE FINDINGS. HE DECLARED...

WHAT WE HAVE LEARNED THUS FAR HAS NOT PROVEN SADDAM HUSSEIN HAD WHAT INTELLIGENCE INDICATED AND WHAT WE BELIEVED HE HAD...BUT IT ALSO HAS NOT PROVEN THE OPPOSITE.

BUT ONE DAY LATER, IN A SPEECH AT GEORGETOWN UNIVERSITY, CIA DIRECTOR TENET ADMITTED THAT THE U.S. "MAY HAVE OVERESTIMATED THE PROGRESS" IRAQ HAD MADE IN ATTAINING NUCLEAR WEAPONS CAPABILITIES.

IN MID-FEBRUARY, DEFENSE DEPARTMENT OFFICIALS DISCLOSED THEIR PLANS TO HOLD A LARGE PORTION OF THE GUANTÁNAMO BAY DETAINEES FOR YEARS, IF NOT INDEFINITELY. "WE ARE IN AN ACTIVE WAR," EXPLAINED ONE OFFICIAL.

A "QUASI PAROLE BOARD" WOULD BE CREATED, THEY SAID, BEFORE WHICH A PRISONER'S CASE COULD BE APPEALED.

DEADLY INSURGENT ATTACKS CONTINUED THROUGHOUT FEBRUARY. INSURGENTS RAIDED THE MAIN FALLUJAH POLICE STATION, KILLING 15 OFFICERS AND FREEING SCORES OF PRISONERS.

IN LATE FEBRUARY, GERMAN AND AMERICAN OFFICIALS DISCLOSED THAT THE NAME AND TELEPHONE NUMBER OF 9/11 HIJACKER MARWIN AL-SHEHHI WAS GIVEN TO THE CIA BY GERMAN INTELLIGENCE IN MARCH 1999. THOUGH THE OFFICIALS SUGGESTED HE BE TRACKED, THE PROPOSAL WAS NOT FOLLOWED THROUGH.

SUICIDE TRUCK BOMBS ASSAULTED A POLISH ARMY-GUARDED BASE NEAR BAGHDAD, KILLING 11 AND WOUNDING MORE THAN 100. AND ON MARCH 2, IN WHAT BECAME THE DEADLIEST DAY SINCE THE U.S. INVASION, BOMBERS AND ATTACKERS KILLED MORE THAN 143 SHIITES AT MOSQUES IN BAGHDAD AND KARBALA.

A GIANT STEP FORWARD WAS TAKEN IN EARLY MARCH WHEN THE 25-MEMBER IRAQI GOVERNING COUNCIL AGREED UNANIMOUSLY TO AN INTERIM CONSTITUTION THAT WOULD SERVE THE GOVERNMENT THROUGH NEXT YEAR.

INCLUDED IN IT WERE MEASURES CALLING FOR EQUAL TREATMENT UNDER LAW, FREEDOM OF SPEECH, PRESS, AND EXCERCISE OF RELIGION, MEASURES THAT COULD MAKE IT THE ARAB WORLD'S MOST LIBERAL DOCUMENT. ALL MEMBERS SIGNED EIGHT DAYS LATER, THOUGH 12 SHIITE DELEGATES PROMISED AMENDMENTS.

HOWEVER, IN ANOTHER PART OF THE WORLD, VIOLENCE EXPLODED ON MARCH 11. IN THE DEADLIEST ATTACK ON A EUROPEAN TARGET SINCE WORLD WAR II, TEN BOMBS WERE SET OFF ON FOUR COMMUTER TRAINS IN MADRID, SPAIN, KILLING AT LEAST 200 PEOPLE AND WOUNDING MORE THAN 1,500.
FIRST BLAMED ON A BASQUE SEPARATIST GROUP, IT SOON EMERGED AS THE WORK OF ISLAMIST TERRORISTS.
THREE DAYS LATER, AS THE DIRECT RESULT OF THE TRAIN DISASTERS, SPAIN'S UNDERDOG SOCIALIST NOMINEE, JOSÉ LUIS RODRÍGUEZ ZAPATERO, SWEPT INTO POWER AS PRIME MINISTER...AND THE NATION'S CONTRIBUTION OF 1,300 TROOPS IN IRAQ WAS IN DANGER OF BEING ENDED.
ON MARCH 16, A PUBLIC OPINION POLL TAKEN BY ABC NEWS AMONG 2,737 IRAQIS FINDS THAT A YEAR AFTER THE AMERICAN-LED INVASION OF THEIR NATION...

- 48% SAY THE U.S. WAS RIGHT TO LEAD INVASION
- 39% SAY IT WAS WRONG
- 13% HAD NO OPINION
- 56% SAY CONDITIONS ARE BETTER THAN BEFORE THE WAR
- 19% SAY CONDITIONS ARE WORSE
- 23% SAY CONDITIONS ARE THE SAME
- 2% HAD NO OPINION

VIOLENCE CONTINUED IN IRAQ. ON MARCH 17, A DEADLY CAR BOMB EXPLODED AND DESTROYED THE FIVE-STORY LE BARON HOTEL IN BAGHDAD, KILLING MORE THAN 27 PEOPLE AND WOUNDING 41. IT WAS KNOWN FOR HOUSING AMERICANS, BRITISH, AND OTHER EUROPEANS.

THE MID-MARCH PUBLICATION OF FORMER COUNTERTERRORISM CHIEF RICHARD CLARKE'S BOOK, *AGAINST ALL ENEMIES*, CAUSED A FUROR WITHIN THE ADMINISTRATION. CLARKE CLAIMED THE PRESIDENT PRESSED HIM ON THREE DIFFERENT OCCASIONS TO FIND EVIDENCE THAT IRAQ WAS BEHIND THE 9/11 ATTACKS. EACH TIME CLARKE REPORTED THERE WAS NONE. CLARKE DESCRIBED ONE SUCH ENCOUNTER...

I WANT YOU, AS SOON AS YOU CAN, TO GO BACK OVER EVERYTHING. *EVERYTHING!*

SEE IF SADDAM DID THIS. SEE IF HE'S LINKED IN ANY WAY.

KA-BLAMM!

THE PRESIDENT SAID HE DID NOT RECALL THE CONVERSATION, THOUGH CLARKE MAINTAINED THERE WERE FOUR WITNESSES.

ON MARCH 24, CLARKE REPEATED THESE CHARGES TO THE 9/11 COMMISSION, ALSO CLAIMING THAT THE ADMINISTRATION HAD LARGELY IGNORED AL QAEDA BEFORE SEPTEMBER 11, 2001. GOP LEADERS TRIED TO DISCREDIT HIS STORY...LIKE SENATE MAJORITY LEADER BILL FRIST...

IT IS ONE THING FOR MR. CLARKE TO DISSEMBLE IN FRONT OF THE MEDIA...BUT IF HE LIED UNDER OATH TO THE UNITED STATES CONGRESS, IT IS A FAR MORE SERIOUS MATTER.

THE BOOK IS THE BOOK. AND YOU CAN READ IT AND MAKE YOUR OWN JUDGMENT AS TO WHETHER IT'S ACCURATE.

SECRETARY OF STATE COLIN POWELL SPOKE DIFFERENTLY.

MR. POWELL CREDITED CLARKE AS "AN EXPERT IN THESE MATTERS" WHO HAD "SERVED HIS NATION VERY, VERY WELL."

ON MARCH 31, TWO CHILLING INCIDENTS RESULTING IN NINE AMERICAN DEATHS TOOK PLACE IN THE DANGEROUS SUNNI TRIANGLE. FOUR SECURITY COMPANY WORKERS WERE AMBUSHED, KILLED, THEN DRAGGED THROUGH THE STREETS OF FALUJAH. FIFTEEN MILES AWAY, FIVE AMERICAN SOLDIERS WERE KILLED WHEN A BOMB EXPLODED NEAR THEIR ARMORED VEHICLE.

"THE INSURGENTS IN FALLUJAH ARE TESTING US," CLAIMED MARINE CAPT. CHRIS LOGAN. "BUT IT'S NOT THAT WE'RE GOING TO LEAVE. WE JUST GOT HERE."

FIVE DAYS LATER, MILITIAS LOYAL TO CLERIC MUQTADA AL-SADR STRUCK IN BAGHDAD'S SADR CITY SLUM, KILLING SEVEN AMERICAN SOLDIERS.

IN NAJAF, 24 PEOPLE WERE KILLED AND 200 WOUNDED IN CLASHES WITH SPANISH-LED COALITION TROOPS.

HOURS AFTER SADR TOLD HIS LOYALISTS TO "TERRORIZE YOUR ENEMY," TENS OF THOUSANDS OF HIS FOLLOWERS APPEARED IN THE STREETS OF SEVERAL CITIES.

WE'RE FACING A TEST OF WILLS AND WE WILL MEET THAT TEST.

THIS WAS THE FIRST TIME SINCE SADDAM HUSSEIN'S FALL A YEAR AGO THAT COALITION FORCES WERE FIGHTING BOTH SUNNI AND SHIITE INSURGENTS. PRESIDENT BUSH SAID THAT AMERICA WOULD NOT BOW TO THE VIOLENCE IN IRAQ.

NO VIOLENCE WE HAVE SEEN IS A POWER GRAB BY THESE EXTREME AND RUTHLESS ELEMENTS. IT'S NOT A CIVIL WAR. IT'S NOT A POPULAR UPRISING.

OVER THE PREVIOUS TWO WEEKS, 86 AMERICAN SERVICE PEOPLE HAD BEEN KILLED AND 561 WOUNDED IN IRAQ.

REPORTER BOB WOODWARD'S *PLAN OF ATTACK* WAS PUBLISHED ON APRIL 16 AND IMMEDIATELY CAUSED AN UPROAR. IN IT HE CLAIMED THAT TWO MONTHS BEFORE THE INVASION OF IRAQ, SECRETARY OF STATE POWELL HAD WARNED PRESIDENT BUSH OF THE POSSIBLE NEGATIVE CONSEQUENCES OF A WAR. MR. POWELL WAS QUOTED AS SAYING ON JANUARY 12, 2003...

...YOU'RE SURE? YOU UNDERSTAND THE CONSEQUENCES? YOU KNOW YOU'RE GOING TO BE *OWNING* THE PLACE?

WOODWARD ALSO CLAIMED THE SECRETARY CLASHED WITH VICE PRESIDENT CHENEY, WHOM THE WRITER DESCRIBED AS A "POWERFUL, STEAM-ROLLING FORCE" PUSHING FOR WAR AND PREOCCUPIED WITH SUPPOSED LINKS BETWEEN AL QAEDA AND SADDAM HUSSEIN.

ON APRIL 18, NEW SPANISH PRIME MINISTER ZAPATERO KEPT HIS CAMPAIGN PROMISE; HE ANNOUNCED THAT ALL 1,300 SPANISH TROOPS WOULD BE COMING HOME...

...AS SOON AS POSSIBLE.

IRAQI INSURGENT VIOLENCE CONTINUED DURING MID-APRIL WITH THREE CAR BOMBINGS AT AN IRAQI POLICE STATION, WITH 20 PEOPLE KILLED AND OVER 60 WOUNDED.

FOLLOWED ONE DAY LATER BY MORTAR FIRE INTO ABU GHRAIB PRISON, KILLING 22 AND WOUNDING 92.

SUPPORT FOR THE IRAQ WAR ERODES. A *NEW YORK TIMES*/CBS POLL IN LATE APRIL FINDS...

47% SAY U.S. IS RIGHT IN TAKING ACTION
58% THOUGHT SO ONE MONTH BEFORE
63% THOUGHT SO IN DECEMBER

PRESIDENT BUSH'S APPROVAL RATE ALSO FALLS
46% APPROVE HIS POLICIES NOW
71% APPROVED HIS POLICIES LAST MARCH
89% APPROVED HIS POLICIES AFTER 9/11 ATTACKS

AT THE END OF APRIL, PHOTOGRAPHS OF AMERICAN SOLDIERS ABUSING NAKED IRAQI PRISONERS IN ABU GHRAIB PRISON SHOCKED AND HORRIFIED THE WORLD. FIRST SHOWN ON CBS'S *60 MINUTES II*, U.S. AND FOREIGN NEWSPAPERS, AS WELL AS AL JAZEERA, THE ARABIC NEWS NETWORK, SOON CARRIED THE IMAGES TO READERS AND VIEWERS EVERYWHERE.

PRESIDENT BUSH QUICKLY VOICED HIS ANGER AND DISMAY.

I SHARED A DEEP DISGUST THAT THESE PRISONERS WERE TREATED THE WAY THEY WERE TREATED.

THEIR TREATMENT DOES NOT REFLECT THE NATURE OF THE AMERICAN PEOPLE.

HE WENT ON TO SAY THAT AN INVESTIGATION WAS MOVING AHEAD.

BRIG. GEN. JANIS KARPINSKI, COMMANDER OF THE ARMY RESERVISTS MILITARY POLICE IN CHARGE OF THE PRISON, CLAIMED SHE ONLY LEARNED OF THE ABUSE WEEKS AFTER IT HAPPENED. RELIEVED OF HER COMMAND AND SENT HOME, SHE POINTED HER FINGER AT MILITARY INTELLIGENCE OFFICERS.

WE'RE DISPOSABLE. WHY WOULD THEY WANT THE ACTIVE-DUTY PEOPLE TO TAKE THE BLAME? THEY WANT TO PUT THIS ON THE MP'S AND HOPE THAT THIS THING GOES AWAY.

ARMY INVESTIGATORS DISCOVERED THAT MIDLEVEL INTELLIGENCE OFFICERS IN ABU GHRAIB WERE ALLOWED TO BYPASS CHAINS OF COMMAND AND ORDER ENLISTED PERSONNEL TO USE QUESTIONABLE METHODS. ALL PRISONS IN IRAQ ARE SOON TO BE INVESTIGATED.

YOU DO WHAT YOU *HAVE* TO, SOLDIER!

BY MAY 3, SIX U.S. SOLDIERS WERE SEVERELY REPRIMANDED AND A SEVENTH RECEIVED A LESSER "LETTER OF ADMONISHMENT."

ON MAY 4, MOST OF IRAQ'S IMPORTANT SHIITE LEADERS CALLED FOR MUQTADA AL-SADR'S FORCES TO WITHDRAW FROM NAJAF AND KARBALA. SADR'S INFLUENCE WAS APPARENTLY DIMINISHED, A REPRESENTATIVE OF AYATOLLAH SISTANI COMMENTED.

HE IS 100% ISOLATED ACROSS MOST OF THE SOUTHERN PROVINCES.

HOURS AFTER THE SHIITE LEADER'S MESSAGE, U.S. TROOPS INSTALLED A NEW GOVERNOR IN NAJAF...

...AND MOVED AGAINST TWO OTHER CITIES.

IN EARLY MAY, AMERICAN GI'S CONTINUED TO BATTLE SADR'S INSURGENTS. CHASING THE CLERIC'S MILITIA, KNOWN AS THE MAHDI ARMY, AMERICANS KILLED 25 INSURGENTS IN KARBALA, 12 IN NAJAF, AND MORE THAN 41 IN KUFA.

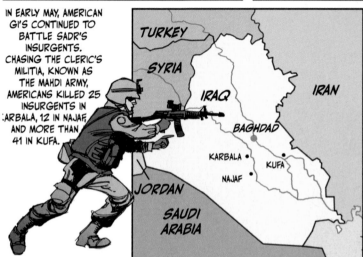

ANSWERING A CALL FOR PEACE, SADR DECLARED: "WHAT KIND OF PEACE COULD COME FROM YOU OR YOUR AGENTS WHEN YOU FEEL THE PLEASURE OF TORTURING PRISONERS?"

DEFENSE SECRETARY RUMSFELD VISITED ABU GHRAIB PRISON ON MAY 13 AND PROMISED...

THE PEOPLE WHO ENGAGED IN ABUSES WILL BE BROUGHT TO JUSTICE. THE WORLD WILL SEE HOW A FREE SYSTEM FUNCTIONS-- TRANSPARENTLY WITH NO COVER-UP.

EZZEDINE SALIM, MAY'S ROTATING PRESIDENT OF THE IRAQI GOVERNING COUNCIL, AND SIX OTHERS WERE KILLED BY A SUICIDE BOMBER NEAR AMERICAN HEADQUARTERS ON MAY 17.

TAKING PLACE 45 DAYS BEFORE AMERICA'S PLANNED PASSING OF LIMITED SOVEREIGNTY OVER TO THE IRAQIS, THIS SEEMED TO ENDANGER THE TRANSFER.

ADDRESSING THE UNITED STATES WAR COLLEGE ON MAY 24, PRESIDENT BUSH DECLARED HIS AIM TO MAKE IRAQIS "FREE, NOT TO MAKE THEM AMERICAN." HE WENT ON...

I SENT AMERICAN TROOPS TO IRAQ TO DEFEND OUR SECURITY, NOT TO STAY AS AN OCCUPYING POWER... IRAQIS WILL MAKE THEIR OWN HISTORY AND FIND THEIR OWN WAY.

AFTER SEVEN WEEKS OF BLOODY BATTLE, ON MAY 27 U.S. FORCES AND SADR'S MAHDI ARMY AGREED TO STOP FIGHTING. IN A PEACE TREATY WORKED OUT BY SADR AND IRAQI LEADERS, A COMPROMISE WAS REACHED KEEPING SADR'S FORCES INTACT BUT OFF THE STREETS.

ON MAY 28 AYAD ALLAWI WAS CHOSEN TO BE IRAQ'S INTERIM PRIME MINISTER IN AN AGREEMENT BETWEEN UN SPECIAL ENVOY LAKHDAR BRAHIMI, AMERICAN OFFICIALS, AND KEY LEADERS.

GEORGE J. TENET, LONGTIME DIRECTOR OF THE CIA, RESIGNS HIS POST ON JUNE 3, CITING PERSONAL REASONS. REPRIMANDS FOR THE CIA'S RECENT WORK, HOWEVER, ARE EXPECTED SHORTLY FROM SEVERAL CONGRESSIONAL COMMITTEES.
HE WILL SERVE UNTIL JULY 11, THE SEVENTH ANNIVERSARY OF HIS TENURE.

THOUGH A MEMBER OF THE IRAQI GOVERNING COUNCIL, DR. ALLAWI WAS A SURPRISE CHOICE. AS ONE COMMENTATOR PUT IT, HE WAS EQUALLY MISTRUSTED BY EVERYONE.
[SEE HTTP://NEWS.BBC.CO.UK/2/HI/MIDDLE_EAST/3757923.STM]

40TH PRESIDENT RONALD REAGAN DIES ON JUNE 5, AT THE AGE OF 93. A FORMER MOVIE STAR, AS PRESIDENT HE LED THE NATION AS SOVIET COMMUNISM COLLAPSED.

IN EARLY JUNE THE UN SECURITY COUNCIL UNANIMOUSLY APPROVED A U.S.-BRITISH RESOLUTION TO END FORMAL OCCUPATION OF IRAQ ON JUNE 30. GRANTING "FULL SOVEREIGNTY" TO AN INTERIM GOVERNMENT, IT CALLED FOR DIRECT ELECTIONS TO APPOINT A FULL-TIME ONE BY DECEMBER 31, 2005. THE WORLD COMMUNITY, SECRETARY OF STATE POWELL DECLARED, "WAS COMING TOGETHER AGAIN TO SUPPORT THE IRAQI PEOPLE."

INSURGENT DEVASTATION NONETHELESS CONTINUED. IN MID-JUNE, AN EXPLOSIVE-FILLED TRUCK WAS PUSHED BY A SUICIDE BOMBER INTO A CONVOY OF FOREIGN CONTRACTORS IN BAGHDAD, KILLING MORE THAN 13 PEOPLE. TWO OTHER BOMBS EXPLODED NORTH AND SOUTH OF THE CAPITAL, KILLING EIGHT MORE.

THE 9/11 COMMISSION REPORT WAS RELEASED ON JUNE 16, FOCUSING NATIONAL ATTENTION ON ITS FINDINGS CONCERNING THE ATTACKS ON SEPTEMBER 11, 2001. THE BIPARTISAN GROUP OF FIVE REPUBLICANS AND FIVE DEMOCRATS FAULTED THE BUSH ADMINISTRATION--AND, TO A LESSER EXTENT, CLINTON'S--AS WELL AS THE FBI, CIA, AND OTHER AGENCIES INVOLVED IN KEEPING THE NATION SAFE. SOME OF THE COMMISSION'S FINDINGS WERE...

LEE H. HAMILTON

WE HAVE NO CREDIBLE EVIDENCE THAT IRAQ AND AL QAEDA COOPERATED IN ATTACKS AGAINST THE UNITED STATES.

JAIME GORELICK

SLADE GORTON

BIN LADIN IS SAID TO HAVE REQUESTED SPACE TO ESTABLISH TRAINING CAMPS AS WELL AS ASSISTANCE IN PROCURING WEAPONS, BUT IRAQ APPARENTLY NEVER RESPONDED.

JOHN F. LEHMAN

RICHARD BEN-VENISTE

FRED F. FIELDING

DESPITE REPORTED CONTACTS BETWEEN AL QAEDA AND IRAQ, THEY DO NOT APPEAR TO HAVE RESULTED IN A COLLABORATIVE RELATIONSHIP.

TIMOTHY J. ROEMER

BOB KERRY

JAMES R. THOMPSON

WE DO NOT BELIEVE SUCH A MEETING [A SUPPOSED MEETING BETWEEN TERRORIST MOHAMED ATTA AND IRAQI INTELLIGENCE IN APRIL 2001] OCCURRED.

TOM KEAN

THERE WERE SYSTEMATIC EFFORTS BY AL QAEDA TO CONNECT WITH IRAQ-- MANY OF THEM FAILED.

NEVERTHELESS, A DAY LATER PRESIDENT BUSH AND VICE PRESIDENT CHENEY INSISTED THAT SADDAM HUSSEIN AND AL QAEDA HAD LONG-STANDING TIES.

THE REASON I KEEP INSISTING THAT THERE WAS A RELATIONSHIP BETWEEN IRAQ AND SADDAM AND AL QAEDA IS BECAUSE THERE *WAS* A RELATIONSHIP BETWEEN IRAQ AND AL QAEDA.

FOR EXAMPLE, IRAQI INTELLIGENCE OFFICERS MET WITH BIN LADIN, THE HEAD OF AL QAEDA, IN THE SUDAN.*

*THE 9/11 COMMISSION REPORTED THAT AN IRAQI INTELLIGENCE OFFICER "MADE THREE VISITS TO SUDAN" IN 1994 WHERE HE MET WITH BIN LADIN, WHO WANTED TO OPEN CAMPS IN IRAQ AND OBTAIN WEAPONS.
"BUT IRAQ APPARENTLY NEVER RESPONDED."

[THE 9/11 COMMISSION] DID NOT ADDRESS THE BROADER QUESTION OF A RELATIONSHIP BETWEEN IRAQ AND AL QAEDA IN OTHER AREAS, IN OTHER WAYS...THE EVIDENCE IS OVERWHELMING.

TOWARD THE END OF JUNE, IRAQI KURDS INCREASINGLY REPOSSESSED LANDS THAT HAD BEEN FORCEFULLY TAKEN FROM THEM BY SADDAM HUSSEIN'S REGIME.
THOUSANDS OF KURDS SWEPT NORTHWARD, SEIZING LAND FROM ARABS WHO HAD SETTLED THERE DURING SADDAM'S YEARS IN POWER, A REGIME, INCIDENTALLY, WHICH TOOK POWER IN 1979.

DISPLACED AND FRIGHTENED ARABS, REPORTED TO BE AS MANY AS 100,000, RETREATED TO CROWDED CAMPS.

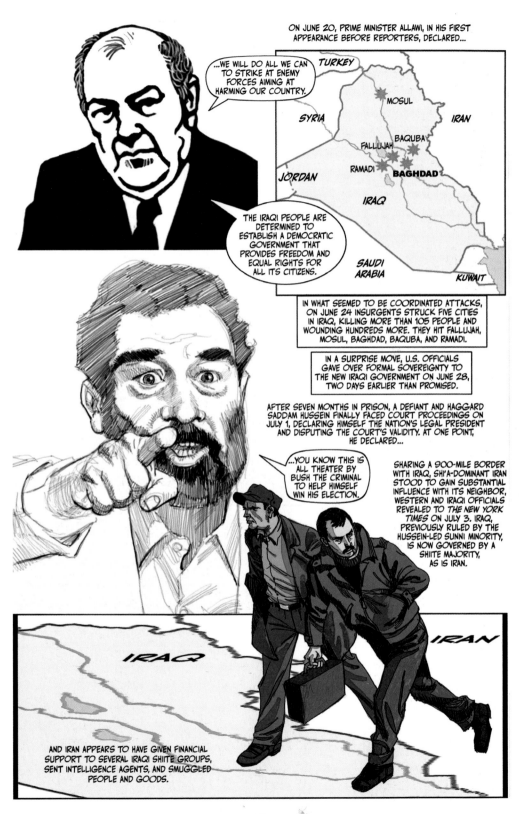

ON JUNE 20, PRIME MINISTER ALLAWI, IN HIS FIRST APPEARANCE BEFORE REPORTERS, DECLARED...

...WE WILL DO ALL WE CAN TO STRIKE AT ENEMY FORCES AIMING AT HARMING OUR COUNTRY.

TURKEY

SYRIA

IRAN

MOSUL

BAQUBA

FALLUJAH

RAMADI   BAGHDAD

JORDAN

IRAQ

THE IRAQI PEOPLE ARE DETERMINED TO ESTABLISH A DEMOCRATIC GOVERNMENT THAT PROVIDES FREEDOM AND EQUAL RIGHTS FOR ALL ITS CITIZENS.

SAUDI ARABIA

KUWAIT

IN WHAT SEEMED TO BE COORDINATED ATTACKS, ON JUNE 24 INSURGENTS STRUCK FIVE CITIES IN IRAQ, KILLING MORE THAN 105 PEOPLE AND WOUNDING HUNDREDS MORE. THEY HIT FALLUJAH, MOSUL, BAGHDAD, BAQUBA, AND RAMADI.

IN A SURPRISE MOVE, U.S. OFFICIALS GAVE OVER FORMAL SOVEREIGNTY TO THE NEW IRAQI GOVERNMENT ON JUNE 28, TWO DAYS EARLIER THAN PROMISED.

AFTER SEVEN MONTHS IN PRISON, A DEFIANT AND HAGGARD SADDAM HUSSEIN FINALLY FACED COURT PROCEEDINGS ON JULY 1, DECLARING HIMSELF THE NATION'S LEGAL PRESIDENT AND DISPUTING THE COURT'S VALIDITY. AT ONE POINT, HE DECLARED...

...YOU KNOW THIS IS ALL THEATER BY BUSH THE CRIMINAL TO HELP HIMSELF WIN HIS ELECTION.

SHARING A 900-MILE BORDER WITH IRAQ, SHI'A-DOMINANT IRAN STOOD TO GAIN SUBSTANTIAL INFLUENCE WITH ITS NEIGHBOR, WESTERN AND IRAQI OFFICIALS REVEALED TO *THE NEW YORK TIMES* ON JULY 3. IRAQ, PREVIOUSLY RULED BY THE HUSSEIN-LED SUNNI MINORITY, IS NOW GOVERNED BY A SHIITE MAJORITY, AS IS IRAN.

IRAQ

IRAN

AND IRAN APPEARS TO HAVE GIVEN FINANCIAL SUPPORT TO SEVERAL IRAQI SHIITE GROUPS, SENT INTELLIGENCE AGENTS, AND SMUGGLED PEOPLE AND GOODS.

HAVING ALREADY WON THE DEMOCRATIC PRESIDENTIAL NOMINATION IN THE PRIMARIES, SENATOR JOHN KERRY NAMED 51-YEAR-OLD NORTH CAROLINA SENATOR JOHN EDWARDS AS HIS VICE-PRESIDENTIAL RUNNING MATE ON JULY 6.

"I HAVE CHOSEN A MAN WHO UNDERSTANDS AND DEFENDS THE VALUES OF AMERICA," DECLARED KERRY.

A BLISTERING REPORT ISSUED BY A UNANIMOUS SENATE INTELLIGENCE COMMITTEE ON JULY 9 CONDEMNED THE ADMINISTRATION'S JUSTIFICATION FOR WAR IN IRAQ AS UNFOUNDED AND UNREASONABLE.

IN ITS 511-PAGE REPORT, THE COMMITTEE OF 9 REPUBLICANS AND 8 DEMOCRATS STRONGLY BLAMED THE CIA AND ITS DIRECTOR, GEORGE TENET, FOR OVERSTATED AND FAULTY INFORMATION.

SENATOR PAT ROBERTS, THE PANEL'S REPUBLICAN CHAIRMAN

"IN THE END, WHAT THE PRESIDENT AND CONGRESS USED TO SEND THE COUNTRY TO WAR WAS INFORMATION PROVIDED BY THE INTELLIGENCE COMMUNITY, AND THAT INFORMATION WAS FLAWED."

SENATOR JOHN D. ROCKEFELLER IV, OF WEST VIRGINIA, TOP PANEL DEMOCRAT

"THIS INTELLIGENCE FAILURE WILL AFFECT OUR NATIONAL SECURITY FOR YEARS TO COME."

SENATE INTELLIGENCE COMMITTEE REPORT

THE BODY OF ASSESSMENTS SHOWED THAT IRAQI MILITARY CAPABILITIES HAD STEADILY DEGRADED FOLLOWING DEFEAT IN THE FIRST GULF WAR IN 1991.

ANALYSTS ALSO BELIEVED THESE CAPABILITIES WOULD CONTINUE TO ERODE AS LONG AS ECONOMIC SANCTIONS REMAINED IN PLACE.

HE WAS A DANGEROUS MAN. THE WORLD IS BETTER OFF WITHOUT SADDAM HUSSEIN IN POWER. AMERICA IS SAFER.

THE RELATIVE TWO-WEEK CALM THAT HAD PREVAILED IN IRAQ SINCE IT REGAINED SOVEREIGNTY WAS BROKEN IN MID-JULY AS...

...A SUICIDE CAR BOMB KILLED AT LEAST 10 PEOPLE AT THE GATES OF THE AMERICAN GREEN ZONE IN BAGHDAD.

AND GOVERNOR OSAMA KASHMOULA OF NINEVEH PROVINCE WAS ASSASSINATED IN A BARRAGE OF BULLETS.

BLAM! BAM!

RAK ATAK!

THE 9/11 COMMISSION MEMBERS GAVE THEIR FINAL REPORT ON JULY 22, WARNING THAT WORSE TERRORIST ATTACKS AWAITED US IF WE DID NOT RESTRUCTURE OUR INTELLIGENCE AGENCIES AND INTENSIFY OUR DIPLOMACY.

A CRITICAL THEME THAT EMERGED THROUGHOUT OUR INQUIRY WAS THE DIFFICULTY OF ANSWERING THE QUESTION: WHO IS IN CHARGE? TOO OFTEN, THE ANSWER IS NO ONE.

IF IRAQ BECOMES A FAILED STATE, IT WILL GO TO THE TOP OF THE LIST OF PLACES THAT ARE BREEDING GROUNDS FOR ATTACKS AGAINST AMERICANS AT HOME.

COMMISSION MEMBER JAMES R. THOMPSON, FORMER REPUBLICAN GOVERNOR OF ILLINOIS

[THE COMMISSION HAS PRODUCED] VERY SOLID RECOMMENDATIONS ABOUT HOW TO MOVE FORWARD, AND I HAVE ASSURED THEM THAT WHEREVER THE GOVERNMENT NEEDS TO ACT, IT WILL.

DEMOCRAT LEE HAMILTON VICE CHAIR

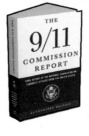

THE 9/11 COMMISSION REPORT

FINAL REPORT OF THE NATIONAL COMMISSION ON TERRORIST ATTACKS UPON THE UNITED STATES

AUTHORIZED EDITION

OUR REFORM RECOMMENDATIONS ARE URGENT...IF THESE REFORMS ARE NOT THE BEST THAT CAN BE DONE FOR THE AMERICAN PEOPLE, THEN CONGRESS AND THE PRESIDENT NEED TO TELL US WHAT'S BETTER.

PRESIDENT GEORGE W. BUSH

AFGHANISTAN   KABUL

KANDAHAR

IN A NEW REPORT, ISSUED ON JULY 23, STUDYING ABUSES AT ABU GHRAIB PRISON IN BAGHDAD, ARMY INSPECTOR GENERAL PAUL T. MIKOLASHEK STATED THAT THE ALLEGED ABUSES WERE CAUSED BY UNAUTHORIZED ACTIONS OF A FEW INDIVIDUALS AND THE FAILURE OF A FEW LEADERS TO PROVIDE APPROPRIATE GUIDANCE.

NOT BY SYSTEMIC PROBLEMS, AS PREVIOUSLY CONCLUDED BY MAJ. GEN. ANTONIO TAGUBA.

TALIBAN ATTACKS IN AFGHANISTAN INTENSIFIED DURING THE PAST MONTHS, AMERICAN COMMANDERS AND AFGHAN OFFICIALS REPORTED TO THE NEW YORK TIMES ON JULY 31. MOST ATTACKS OCCURRED ALONG THE 1,500-MILE PAKISTANI BORDER AND NEAR KANDAHAR IN THE SOUTH.

THUS FAR IN 2005, 23 AMERICAN TROOPS HAD DIED FROM HOSTILE FIRE, WHILE 12 WERE KILLED IN ALL OF 2003.

IN EARLY AUGUST, CAR BOMBS WERE EXPLODED NEAR FOUR BAGHDAD CHURCHES AND ONE IN MOSUL IN THE FIRST PORTENTOUS ATTACKS AGAINST IRAQI CHRISTIANS.
AT LEAST 11 DIED IN BAGHDAD AND 1 IN MOSUL, WHILE MANY MORE WERE WOUNDED.

HURRICANE CHARLEY SMASHES FLORIDA'S WEST COAST IN MID-AUGUST WITH WINDS OF 145 MPH, CAUSING NEARLY 2 MILLION PEOPLE TO EVACUATE THEIR HOMES. DAMAGE IS ESTIMATED AT $17 BILLION WITH TENS OF THOUSANDS LEFT HOMELESS AND ALMOST 3 MILLION PEOPLE LEFT WITHOUT POWER.

AFTER A TWO-WEEK BATTLE BETWEEN U.S. TROOPS AND FOLLOWERS OF THE REBEL SHIITE CLERIC MUQTADA AL-SADR AROUND THE IMAM ALI SHRINE AT NAJAF, PRIME MINISTER ALLAWI GAVE THE CLERIC A FINAL WARNING ON AUGUST 19 TO DISARM AND LEAVE THE SHRINE.

ON AUGUST 24, AN INDEPENDENT PANEL HEADED BY FORMER DEFENSE SECRETARY AND FORMER DIRECTOR OF THE CIA JAMES R. SCHLESINGER BLAMED MILITARY OFFICIALS ALL THE WAY TO "HIGHER LEVELS" FOR ABUSES AT ABU GHRAIB AND IN METHODS OF PRISONER INTERROGATION. SAID SCHLESINGER...

...THERE IS BOTH INSTITUTIONAL AND PERSONAL RESPONSIBILITY AT HIGHER LEVELS.

WHILE DEFENSE SECRETARY RUMSFELD STATED...

...THE DEFENSE DEPARTMENT HAS AN OBLIGATION TO EVALUATE WHAT HAPPENED AND TO MAKE APPROPRIATE CHANGES.

ON AUGUST 27, THE THREE-WEEK SIEGE AT IMAM ALI SHRINE WAS FINALLY ENDED.

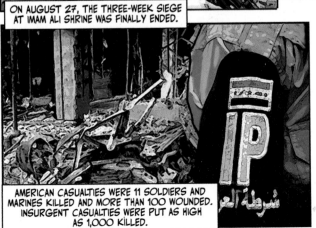

AMERICAN CASUALTIES WERE 11 SOLDIERS AND MARINES KILLED AND MORE THAN 100 WOUNDED. INSURGENT CASUALTIES WERE PUT AS HIGH AS 1,000 KILLED.

AMERICAN MILITARY DEATHS IN IRAQ PASSED THE 1,000 MARK, THE DEFENSE DEPARTMENT ACKNOWLEDGED ON SEPTEMBER 7. THE PENTAGON ALSO CONCEDED THAT INSURGENTS CONTROLLED MANY IMPORTANT REGIONS IN THE COUNTRY, AND ACCORDING TO RICHARD B. MYERS, CHAIRMAN OF THE JOINT CHIEFS OF STAFF, THEY WOULD NOT BE CONFRONTED UNTIL THE END OF THE YEAR.
FOUR OF THE INSURGENT-CONTROLLED CITIES WERE RAMADI, FALLUJAH, BAQUBA, AND SAMARRA, ALL IN THE SO-CALLED SUNNI TRIANGLE.

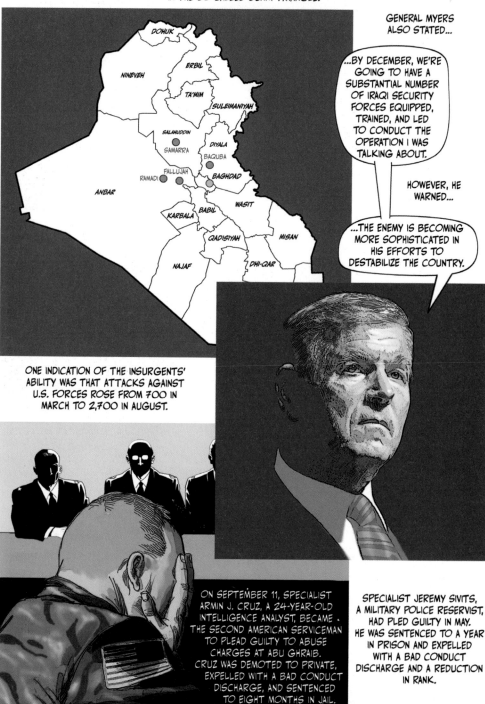

GENERAL MYERS ALSO STATED...

...BY DECEMBER, WE'RE GOING TO HAVE A SUBSTANTIAL NUMBER OF IRAQI SECURITY FORCES EQUIPPED, TRAINED, AND LED TO CONDUCT THE OPERATION I WAS TALKING ABOUT.

HOWEVER, HE WARNED...

...THE ENEMY IS BECOMING MORE SOPHISTICATED IN HIS EFFORTS TO DESTABILIZE THE COUNTRY.

ONE INDICATION OF THE INSURGENTS' ABILITY WAS THAT ATTACKS AGAINST U.S. FORCES ROSE FROM 700 IN MARCH TO 2,700 IN AUGUST.

ON SEPTEMBER 11, SPECIALIST ARMIN J. CRUZ, A 24-YEAR-OLD INTELLIGENCE ANALYST, BECAME THE SECOND AMERICAN SERVICEMAN TO PLEAD GUILTY TO ABUSE CHARGES AT ABU GHRAIB. CRUZ WAS DEMOTED TO PRIVATE, EXPELLED WITH A BAD CONDUCT DISCHARGE, AND SENTENCED TO EIGHT MONTHS IN JAIL.

SPECIALIST JEREMY SIVITS, A MILITARY POLICE RESERVIST, HAD PLED GUILTY IN MAY. HE WAS SENTENCED TO A YEAR IN PRISON AND EXPELLED WITH A BAD CONDUCT DISCHARGE AND A REDUCTION IN RANK.

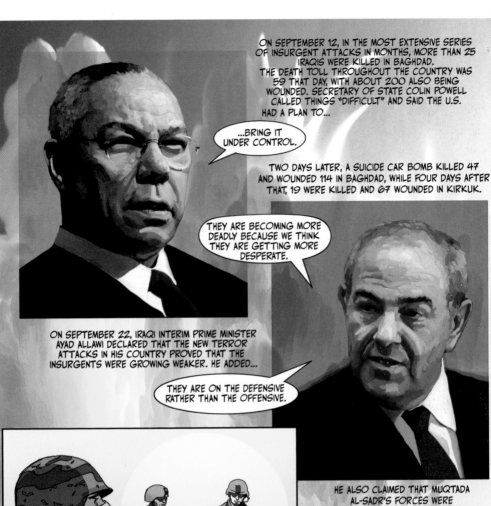

ON SEPTEMBER 12, IN THE MOST EXTENSIVE SERIES OF INSURGENT ATTACKS IN MONTHS, MORE THAN 25 IRAQIS WERE KILLED IN BAGHDAD.
THE DEATH TOLL THROUGHOUT THE COUNTRY WAS 59 THAT DAY, WITH ABOUT 200 ALSO BEING WOUNDED. SECRETARY OF STATE COLIN POWELL CALLED THINGS "DIFFICULT" AND SAID THE U.S. HAD A PLAN TO...

...BRING IT UNDER CONTROL.

TWO DAYS LATER, A SUICIDE CAR BOMB KILLED 47 AND WOUNDED 114 IN BAGHDAD, WHILE FOUR DAYS AFTER THAT, 19 WERE KILLED AND 67 WOUNDED IN KIRKUK.

THEY ARE BECOMING MORE DEADLY BECAUSE WE THINK THEY ARE GETTING MORE DESPERATE.

ON SEPTEMBER 22, IRAQI INTERIM PRIME MINISTER AYAD ALLAWI DECLARED THAT THE NEW TERROR ATTACKS IN HIS COUNTRY PROVED THAT THE INSURGENTS WERE GROWING WEAKER. HE ADDED...

THEY ARE ON THE DEFENSIVE RATHER THAN THE OFFENSIVE.

HE ALSO CLAIMED THAT MUQTADA AL-SADR'S FORCES WERE "DISINTEGRATING."

DURING SEPTEMBER, MORE THAN 2,300 ATTACKS BY INSURGENTS IN IRAQ--OVER AN AREA FROM NINEVEH TO BABYLON TO BASRA-- SEEMED TO CONTRADICT ALLAWI AND THREATEN THE SCHEDULED JANUARY ELECTIONS.

ON OCTOBER 6, A REPORT ISSUED BY CHIEF U.S. WEAPONS INSPECTOR CHARLES A. DUELFER DECLARED THAT IRAQ HAD "ESSENTIALLY DESTROYED" ITS ILLICIT WEAPONS STOCKPILES IN 1991, AND NO EVIDENCE HAD BEEN FOUND OF ANY EFFORT TO REINTRODUCE THE PROGRAM.
DEMOCRATIC SENATOR JOHN D. ROCKEFELLER QUICKLY RESPONDED...

WE INVADED A COUNTRY, THOUSANDS OF PEOPLE HAVE DIED, AND IRAQ NEVER POSED A GRAVE OR GROWING DANGER.

AN ARMY RESERVE PLATOON OF 18 MEN AND WOMEN REFUSED TO DELIVER A FUEL SHIPMENT FROM NASRIYA TO A BASE FARTHER NORTH ON OCTOBER 13.

THEY DEEMED THEIR TRUCKS UNSAFE AND WITHOUT ADEQUATE PROTECTION.

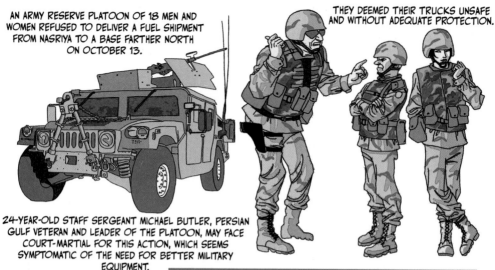

24-YEAR-OLD STAFF SERGEANT MICHAEL BUTLER, PERSIAN GULF VETERAN AND LEADER OF THE PLATOON, MAY FACE COURT-MARTIAL FOR THIS ACTION, WHICH SEEMS SYMPTOMATIC OF THE NEED FOR BETTER MILITARY EQUIPMENT.

AN ESTIMATED 208 IRAQIS WERE KILLED DURING THE WEEK OF OCTOBER 11-17 BY WAR-RELATED CAUSES. DURING THAT PERIOD, 23 U.S. MEMBERS OF THE ARMED FORCES ALSO DIED.

MONDAY................... 12

TUESDAY................ 46

WEDNESDAY............ 10

THURSDAY............ 58

FRIDAY................... 24

SATURDAY............. 31

SUNDAY.................. 27

THE INSURGENCY SEEMED TO GROW AS 18 IRAQIS WERE KILLED AND DOZENS WOUNDED IN SEVERAL ATTACKS BY GUERRILLAS ON OCTOBER 23. THE FOLLOWING DAY, 50 NEWLY-TRAINED IRAQI SOLDIERS WERE KILLED EXECUTION-STYLE BY INSURGENTS DRESSED AS POLICEMEN.

IT BECAME APPARENT ON OCTOBER 25 THAT HAMID KARZAI HAD WON THE ELECTION, SECURING HIS POSITION AS AFGHANISTAN'S FIRST POPULARLY ELECTED PRESIDENT.

WINNING MORE THAN 8.7 MILLION POPULAR VOTES AND MANY MORE ELECTORAL VOTES THAN HE DID IN 2000, GEORGE W. BUSH WON A SECOND TERM AS PRESIDENT ON NOVEMBER 2 AGAINST SENATOR JOHN KERRY.

THOUGH RECEIVING OVER 50% OF THE APPROXIMATELY 8 MILLION VOTES CAST, IT WAS NOT THE LANDSLIDE HE AND HIS AMERICAN BACKERS HAD HOPED FOR.

REPUBLICANS ALSO ADDED TO THEIR MAJORITIES IN BOTH HOUSES OF CONGRESS. PROMISED MR. BUSH...

...WE WILL HELP THE EMERGING DEMOCRACIES OF IRAQ AND AFGHANISTAN SO THEY CAN GROW IN STRENGTH AND DEFEND THEIR FREEDOM.

ON NOVEMBER 5, GOVERNMENT OFFICIALS ESTIMATED THAT 6,000 SURFACE-TO-AIR MISSILES WERE MISSING FROM IRAQ'S ARSENAL AND SAID THEY WERE NOT SURE WHEN THE DISAPPEARANCE OCCURRED.

THESE SHOULDER-LAUNCHING WEAPONS HAVE BEEN USED SUCCESSFULLY AGAINST AIRCRAFT. SECRETARY OF STATE POWELL DECLARED, "NO THREAT IS MORE SERIOUS TO AVIATION" THAN THIS.

PALESTINIAN PRESIDENT YASSER ARAFAT DIES IN A PARIS HOSPITAL ON NOVEMBER 10 AT THE AGE OF 75. HE HAD LINGERED IN A COMA FOR DAYS FROM AN UNNAMED DISEASE. HE IS BURIED TWO DAYS LATER IN RAMALLAH ON THE WEST BANK AS 20,000 MOURNERS SURROUND THE COFFIN.

AFTER A WEEKLONG BATTLE, 15,000 AMERICAN AND IRAQI TROOPS OVERCAME INSURGENT RESISTANCE IN FALLUJAH, ON NOVEMBER 14, AS THE CITY LAY IN RUINS. "WE'RE SWEEPING THE CITY NOW," DECLARED MARINE MAJ. GEN. RICHARD NATONSKI. "WE'RE CLEARING OUT POCKETS OF RESISTANCE."

THIRTY-EIGHT AMERICAN SERVICE MEMBERS DIED AND 275 WERE WOUNDED IN THIS ACTION, WHILE IT IS ESTIMATED THAT 1,200 TO 1,600 INSURGENTS WERE KILLED.

COLIN POWELL ANNOUNCED HIS RESIGNATION BY "MUTUAL AGREEMENT" WITH THE PRESIDENT ON NOVEMBER 15. HE WOULD REMAIN IN OFFICE UNTIL THE END OF THE YEAR, WHEN NATIONAL SECURITY ADVISER CONDOLEEZZA RICE SUCCEEDED HIM.

A GROUP OF THE WORLD'S LARGEST INDUSTRIAL COUNTRIES AGREED ON NOVEMBER 21 TO CANCEL 80% OF IRAQ'S $39 BILLION DEBT. IT WAS DONE WITH THE HOPE THAT OTHER NATIONS WOULD DO LIKEWISE AND HELP IRAQ'S RECOVERY. U.S. TREASURY SECRETARY JOHN SNOW SAID...

THIS IS A REAL MILESTONE AND SHOWS THAT THE TRANSATLANTIC ALLIANCE REMAINS A STRONG FORCE FOR GOOD IN THE WORLD.

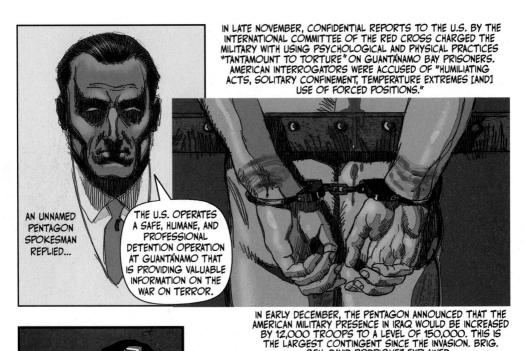

IN LATE NOVEMBER, CONFIDENTIAL REPORTS TO THE U.S. BY THE INTERNATIONAL COMMITTEE OF THE RED CROSS CHARGED THE MILITARY WITH USING PSYCHOLOGICAL AND PHYSICAL PRACTICES "TANTAMOUNT TO TORTURE" ON GUANTÁNAMO BAY PRISONERS. AMERICAN INTERROGATORS WERE ACCUSED OF "HUMILIATING ACTS, SOLITARY CONFINEMENT, TEMPERATURE EXTREMES [AND] USE OF FORCED POSITIONS."

AN UNNAMED PENTAGON SPOKESMAN REPLIED...

THE U.S. OPERATES A SAFE, HUMANE, AND PROFESSIONAL DETENTION OPERATION AT GUANTÁNAMO THAT IS PROVIDING VALUABLE INFORMATION ON THE WAR ON TERROR.

IN EARLY DECEMBER, THE PENTAGON ANNOUNCED THAT THE AMERICAN MILITARY PRESENCE IN IRAQ WOULD BE INCREASED BY 12,000 TROOPS TO A LEVEL OF 150,000. THIS IS THE LARGEST CONTINGENT SINCE THE INVASION. BRIG. GEN. DAVID RODRIGUEZ EXPLAINED...

IT'S MAINLY TO PROVIDE SECURITY FOR THE ELECTIONS, BUT IT'S ALSO TO KEEP UP THE PRESSURE ON THE INSURGENCY.

10,400 SERVICE PEOPLE WILL HAVE THEIR TOURS EXTENDED, MANY FOR A SECOND TIME.

A THREE-DAY SERIES OF ATTACKS BY INSURGENTS, FROM DECEMBER 3 TO DECEMBER 5, KILLED MORE THAN 80 IRAQIS AND THREATENED THE SCHEDULED JANUARY ELECTIONS.

THE HOUSE ARMED SERVICES COMMITTEE ON DECEMBER 9 RELEASED DATA SHOWING SEVERE SHORTAGES OF ARMOR ON MILITARY TRUCKS IN IRAQ. ONLY 10% OF MEDIUM-WEIGHT TRANSPORT TRUCKS AND 15% OF HEAVY-WEIGHT ONES HAD ARMOR.

PRESIDENT BUSH COUNTERED...

...I HAVE TOLD MANY FAMILIES I'VE MET WITH THAT WE'RE DOING EVERYTHING WE CAN TO PROTECT YOUR LOVED ONES ON A MISSION WHICH IS VITAL AND IMPORTANT.

SWORN IN LAST WEEK AS AFGHANISTAN'S FIRST POPULARLY ELECTED PRESIDENT, HAMID KARZAI DECLARED ON DECEMBER 12 THAT HE WOULD DESTROY THE NATION'S THRIVING POPPY FIELDS WITHIN TWO YEARS. SAID KARZAI...

...IT HURTS OUR ECONOMY, IT DESTROYS OUR GOVERNMENT, IT BRINGS US A BAD NAME.

AFGHANISTAN PRODUCES 87% OF THE WORLD'S OPIUM.

AT LEAST 16 IRAQIS WERE KILLED AND 120 WOUNDED AS INSURGENTS STRUCK NAJAF, KARBALA, AND BAGHDAD WITH CAR BOMBS, GRENADES, AND MACHINE-GUN FIRE ON DECEMBER 19. SHIITE CLERICS BLAMED THE ATTACKS ON SUNNI FANATICS ATTEMPTING TO DELAY JANUARY ELECTIONS, ONLY SIX WEEKS AWAY.

A TRUCK BOMB EXPLODED NEAR THE U.S. COMPOUND KILLING 10 AND WOUNDING 60. FIVE AMERICAN SOLDIERS DIED IN THREE OTHER BOMBINGS.

IN A PRESS CONFERENCE ON DECEMBER 20, PRESIDENT BUSH ADMITTED TO ONLY "MIXED" SUCCESS IN TRAINING AN IRAQI ARMY. HE WOULD NOT ARGUE WITH REPUBLICAN SENATOR JOHN WARNER'S ASSESSMENT THAT THESE FORCES WERE AT "BOTTOM LEVEL" AND WITHOUT EFFECTIVE LEADERSHIP. HOWEVER, HE DEFENDED DEFENSE SECRETARY RUMSFELD, SAYING...

...[HE IS] A GOOD HUMAN BEING WHO CARES DEEPLY ABOUT THE MILITARY AND ABOUT THE GRIEF THAT WAR CAUSES.

FBI DOCUMENTS RELEASED ON DECEMBER 20 DEPICT PRISONER ABUSE BY THE U.S. MILITARY IN GUANTÁNAMO AND IRAQ. DESCRIPTIONS OF SUCH TACTICS AS BEATING AND CHOKING DETAINEES, PLACING LIT CIGARETTES IN THEIR EARS, AND FORCING THEM TO URINATE AND DEFECATE ON THEMSELVES WERE PRESENTED AS PART OF A LAWSUIT FILED BY THE ACLU.

RAK-A-TAK!

BAGHDAD PROVINCE GOVERNOR ALI AL-HAIDARI WAS ASSASSINATED ON JANUARY 4 AS INSURGENTS CONTINUED TO THREATEN IRAQI ELECTIONS WITH A SERIES OF VIOLENT ATTACKS.

MICHAEL CHERTOFF WAS NOMINATED BY PRESIDENT BUSH ON JANUARY 10 TO REPLACE TOM RIDGE AS HOMELAND SECURITY SECRETARY. CHERTOFF, WHOSE CONFIRMATION SEEMED ASSURED, WAS A FEDERAL APPEALS JUDGE WHO PRECIOUSLY HELPED LEAD ANTITERRORISM EFFORTS IN THE JUSTICE DEPARTMENT AFTER 9/11. SAID CHERTOFF...

I WILL BE PROUD TO STAND AGAIN WITH THE MEN AND WOMEN WHO FORM OUR FRONT LINE AGAINST TEROR.

ON JANUARY 15, ARMY RESERVIST SPECIALIST CHARLES A. GRANER JR., FOUND GUILTY AS RINGLEADER OF THE ABU GHRAIB ABUSES, WAS SENTENCED TO TEN YEARS IN A MILITARY PRISON FOR HIS CRIMES. HE WAS ALSO REDUCED IN RANK TO PRIVATE AND DISHONORABLY DISCHARGED. GRANER DECLARED...

IT'S THE HIGHER-UPS THAT SHOULD BE TRIED. THEY LET THE LITTLE GUYS TAKE THE FALL FOR THEM. BUT THE TRUTH WILL COME OUT EVENTUALLY.

FIVE SEPARATE DEVASTATING BOMB ATTACKS BY INSURGENTS IN BAGHDAD KILLED 26 IRAQIS AND WOUNDED MANY MORE ON JANUARY 19. AT LEAST 9 OF THE FATALITIES WERE PART OF THE NEW IRAQI SECURITY FORCE.

UNNAMED AMERICAN COMMANDERS FEAR THAT EVENTS LIKE THIS CAN KEEP FORCES IN IRAQ FOR YEARS.

GEORGE W. BUSH WAS SWORN IN FOR HIS SECOND TERM AS PRESIDENT OF THE UNITED STATES ON JANUARY 20, 2005, DECLARING THAT SPREADING LIBERTY IS THE "CALLING OF OUR TIME." AN ESTIMATED 100,000 PEOPLE ATTENDED THE INAUGURATION, INCLUDING FORMER PRESIDENTS CARTER, BUSH, AND CLINTON.

ON JANUARY 26, A MARINE HELICOPTER CRASHED DURING A DESERT SANDSTORM IN IRAQ, KILLING ALL 31 ON BOARD. ON THAT SAME DAY, 6 OTHER SERVICE PEOPLE DIED IN COMBAT, MAKING THIS THE DEADLIEST DAY FOR U.S. TROOPS SINCE THE INVASION BEGAN. INSURGENTS CONTINUED THEIR VIOLENT CAMPAIGN TO PREVENT THE SCHEDULED ELECTIONS, KILLING 13 AND WOUNDING 40 IN A SERIES OF ATTACKS.

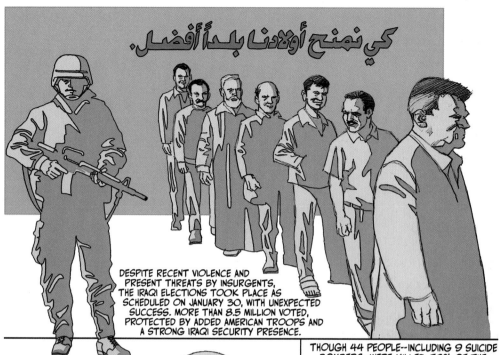

كي نمنح أولادنا بلداً أفضل.

DESPITE RECENT VIOLENCE AND PRESENT THREATS BY INSURGENTS, THE IRAQI ELECTIONS TOOK PLACE AS SCHEDULED ON JANUARY 30, WITH UNEXPECTED SUCCESS. MORE THAN 8.5 MILLION VOTED, PROTECTED BY ADDED AMERICAN TROOPS AND A STRONG IRAQI SECURITY PRESENCE.

THOUGH 44 PEOPLE--INCLUDING 9 SUICIDE BOMBERS--WERE KILLED, 58% OF THE POPULATION WENT TO THE POLLS IN THE NATION'S FIRST FREE ELECTIONS IN 50 YEARS.

THE FINAL ELECTION RESULTS, GIVEN TWO WEEKS LATER, GAVE THE SHIITE ALLIANCE OF RELIGIOUS-POLITICAL PARTIES A SLIM MAJORITY OF 140 SEATS IN THE 275-MEMBER NATIONAL ASSEMBLY. THIS DIMINISHED THE CHANCE FOR A SHIITE THEOCRACY. THE RESULTS WERE...

SHIITE ALLIANCE 140 SEATS

KURDISH PARTIES 75 SEATS

ALLAWI 40 SEATS

OTHERS 20 SEATS

PRESIDENT BUSH NOMINATED JOHN NEGROPONTE AS THE FIRST DIRECTOR OF NATIONAL INTELLIGENCE ON FEBRUARY 17.
CERTAIN OF CONFIRMATION, NEGROPONTE, WHO HAD SERVED EVERY PRESIDENT SINCE JOHN F. KENNEDY, WOULD NOW OVERSEE BOTH CIVILIAN AND MILITARY INTELLIGENCE AGENCIES.

DESPITE THE IRAQI ELECTIONS, INSURGENTS BEGAN A NEW REIGN OF TERROR LASTING THROUGHOUT FEBRUARY.
THE WORST ATTACK--AND THE DEADLIEST SINCE THE AMERICAN INVASION--OCCURRED ON FEBRUARY 28, WHEN A SUICIDE BOMBER EXPLODED HIS SEDAN IN A LARGE CROWD OF POLICE AND ARMY RECRUITS SOUTH OF BAGHDAD, KILLING MORE THAN 122 PEOPLE.

A JUDGE AND HIS LAWYER SON ATTACHED TO THE TRIBUNAL TO TRY SADDAM HUSSEIN WERE ASSASSINATED ON MARCH 1.
THEY WERE KILLED OUTSIDE THEIR HOME BY THREE MEN FIRING AUTOMATIC WEAPONS AS THEIR CAR SPED AWAY.
THE OTHER TRIBUNAL MEMBERS, THEIR NAMES KEPT SECRET, WERE ALL GIVEN SECURITY GUARDS.

ON MARCH 7, A *NEW YORK TIMES* STUDY FOUND THAT THERE HAD BEEN IMPORTANT PENTAGON MISSTEPS IN PROVIDING PROTECTIVE GEAR FOR TROOPS IN IRAQ. THIS INCLUDED BULLETPROOF VESTS, ARMOR FOR HUMVEES, AND ASSORTED ELECTRONIC DEVICES.
MAJ. GEN. ROBERT SCALES JR., FORMER ARMY WAR COLLEGE HEAD, COMMENTED... "...THIS IS A NEW AGE IN WAR WITH AN ENEMY THAT ADAPTS FASTER THAN WE DO."

IN MID-MARCH, ITALIAN PRIME MINISTER SILVIO BERLUSCONI SAID THAT HIS COUNTRY WOULD START WITH-DRAWING ITS 3,000 TROOPS FROM IRAQ BY SEPTEMBER.

ANTIWAR SENTIMENT HAD SWEPT THAT NATION SINCE AN ITALIAN INTELLIGENCE AGENT WAS ACCIDENTALLY KILLED BY U.S. FIRE ON MARCH 4.

ARMY AND NAVY INVESTIGATORS DECLARED ON MARCH 15 THAT THE DEATHS OF AS MANY AS 26 WAR PRISONERS IN CUSTODY MAY HAVE BEEN THE RESULT OF MILITARY HOMICIDE.
THESE DEATHS OCCURRED IN BOTH IRAQ AND AFGHANISTAN, WITH ONLY ONE TAKING PLACE IN ABU GHRAIB.

A PRESIDENTIAL COMMISSION DEALING WITH INTELLIGENCE LAPSES LEADING TO THE IRAQI INVASION CRITICIZED THE CIA UNDER GEORGE TENET, AS WELL AS OTHER AGENCIES, FOR THEIR ERRONEOUS ASSESSMENTS OF SADDAM HUSSEIN'S WEAPONS.
HEADED BY FEDERAL JUDGE LAURENCE SILBERMAN AND FORMER VIRGINIA GOVERNOR CHARLES S. ROBB, THE NINE-MEMBER COMMISSION ALSO APPEARED TO BLAME THE ADMINISTRATION FOR LEADING THE CIA INTO ITS CONCLUSIONS. SAID THE REPORT: "IT IS HARD TO DENY THE CONCLUSION THAT INTELLIGENCE ANALYSTS DID NOT ENCOURAGE SKEPTICISM ABOUT THE CONVENTIONAL WISDOM."

POPE JOHN PAUL II DIES ON APRIL 2 AT THE AGE OF 84, HAVING SERVED FOR 26 YEARS. ONE WEEK LATER, 78-YEAR-OLD GERMAN CARDINAL JOSEPH RATZINGER, A CLOSE ALLY OF JOHN PAUL II, IS CHOSEN THE 265TH POPE AND SELECTS THE NAME OF BENEDICT XVI.

ON APRIL 2, IN THE WAR'S LARGEST ASSAULT ON ABU GHRAIB PRISON, 40 TO 60 INSURGENTS ARMED WITH SUICIDE CAR BOMBS AND VARIOUS WEAPONRY WOUNDED MORE THAN 20 AMERICANS IN THEIR ATTEMPT TO FREE PRISONERS. APACHE HELICOPTERS AND A MARINE COMPANY HELPED SOLDIERS REPEL THE ATTACK IN A 40-MINUTE BATTLE.

AFTER A TWO-MONTH DEADLOCK, ON APRIL 5, IRAQ'S POLITICAL PARTIES CHOSE AS PRESIDENT KURDISH LEADER JALAL TALABANI AND SHIITE ADEL ABDUL MAHDI AND SUNNI SHEIKH GHAZI AL-YAWAR AS VICE PRESIDENTS...

...AND, ONE DAY LATER, APPOINTED SHIITE IBRAHIM AL-JAAFARI AS PRIME MINISTER. JAAFARI, WHO HAD LIVED IN IRAN FOR 20 YEARS, HAD VOICED SUPPORT FOR A STRONG ISLAMIC PRESENCE IN THE GOVERNMENT.

ZACARIAS MOUSSAOUI, THE LONE CAPTURED 9/11 TERRORIST SUSPECT, PLEADED GUILTY ON APRIL 22 TO PARTICIPATING IN AN AL QAEDA PLOT TO FLY PLANES INTO U.S. BUILDINGS.

HOWEVER, HE INSISTED THAT THIS HAD NOTHING TO DO WITH THE 9/11 ATTACKS.

ON APRIL 22, FOUR OF THE FIVE TOP ARMY OFFICERS HEADING IRAQI PRISON OPERATIONS WERE ABSOLVED OF ANY CHARGES OF ABUSE BY AN ARMY INVESTIGATION HEADED BY THE INSPECTOR GENERAL, LT. GEN. STANLEY E. GREEN.

ONLY BRIG. GEN. JANIS KARPINSKY, LEADER OF THE MILITARY POLICE AT ABU GHRAIB, WAS REBUKED AND RELIEVED OF COMMAND. SHE OFTEN COMPLAINED OF BEING MADE THE SCAPEGOAT FOR THESE FAILURES.

AN APRIL 25 REPORT IN *THE NEW YORK TIMES* DESCRIBED THE LACK OF SUPPLIES AND MANPOWER OF MARINE COMPANY E AS AN EXAMPLE OF WHAT WAS TAKING PLACE IN IRAQ.

THIS COMPANY, WITH ONE THIRD OF ITS 185 TROOPS KILLED OR WOUNDED, HAD THE HIGHEST CASUALTY RATE IN THE WAR.

BREAKING THE USUAL CODE OF SILENCE, RETURNING MILITARY PERSONNEL SPOKE OF HUMVEES LACKING APPROPRIATE ARMOR, RESORTING TO CARDBOARD CUTOUTS WITH CAMOUFLAGE SHIRTS TO GIVE THE APPEARANCE OF MORE TROOPS, HOLDING DOORS SHUT BY HAND AS THEY TRAVELED, SCROUNGING FOR METAL FOR PROTECTION, AND SUFFERING AN OVERALL LOSS OF MORALE.

ON APRIL 28, ALMOST THREE MONTHS AFTER NATIONWIDE ELECTIONS, THE NEW IRAQI NATIONAL ASSEMBLY OVERWHELMINGLY APPROVED A SHIITE-LED CABINET. FIVE KEY POSTS WERE STILL TO BE FILLED.

IN RESPONSE TO THIS PROGRESS, A DEVASTATING ARRAY OF ATTACKS BY INSURGENTS OCCURRED FROM LATE APRIL THROUGH THE FIRST WEEK OF MAY.

TWELVE CAR BOMBS ACROSS BAGHDAD KILLED 40+ AND WOUNDED 100+ ON APRIL 29.

THIRTY-FIVE KILLED AND 80 WOUNDED IN AN ATTACK ON KURDS ON MAY 1.

SIXTY KURDS KILLED AND 150 WOUNDED BY A SUICIDE BOMBER ON MAY 3.

TWENTY-TWO KILLED AT AN IRAQI ARMY BASE BY A SUICIDE BOMBER ON MAY 5.

TWENTY-SIX WERE KILLED AND 48 WOUNDED AS A SUICIDE BOMBER STRUCK A BAGHDAD PUBLIC MARKET ON MAY 6.

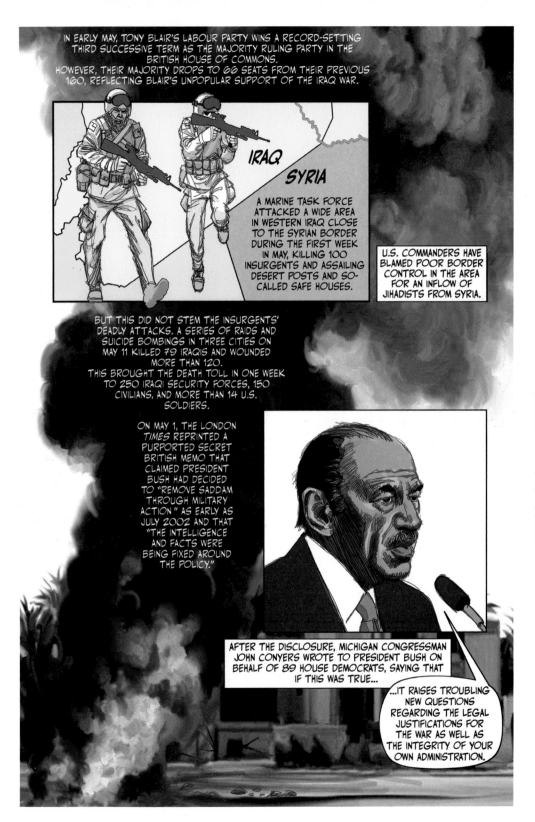

IN EARLY MAY, TONY BLAIR'S LABOUR PARTY WINS A RECORD-SETTING THIRD SUCCESSIVE TERM AS THE MAJORITY RULING PARTY IN THE BRITISH HOUSE OF COMMONS.
HOWEVER, THEIR MAJORITY DROPS TO 66 SEATS FROM THEIR PREVIOUS 160, REFLECTING BLAIR'S UNPOPULAR SUPPORT OF THE IRAQ WAR.

IRAQ

SYRIA

A MARINE TASK FORCE ATTACKED A WIDE AREA IN WESTERN IRAQ CLOSE TO THE SYRIAN BORDER DURING THE FIRST WEEK IN MAY, KILLING 100 INSURGENTS AND ASSAILING DESERT POSTS AND SO-CALLED SAFE HOUSES.

U.S. COMMANDERS HAVE BLAMED POOR BORDER CONTROL IN THE AREA FOR AN INFLOW OF JIHADISTS FROM SYRIA.

BUT THIS DID NOT STEM THE INSURGENTS' DEADLY ATTACKS. A SERIES OF RAIDS AND SUICIDE BOMBINGS IN THREE CITIES ON MAY 11 KILLED 79 IRAQIS AND WOUNDED MORE THAN 120.
THIS BROUGHT THE DEATH TOLL IN ONE WEEK TO 250 IRAQI SECURITY FORCES, 150 CIVILIANS, AND MORE THAN 14 U.S. SOLDIERS.

ON MAY 1, THE LONDON TIMES REPRINTED A PURPORTED SECRET BRITISH MEMO THAT CLAIMED PRESIDENT BUSH HAD DECIDED TO "REMOVE SADDAM THROUGH MILITARY ACTION" AS EARLY AS JULY 2002 AND THAT "THE INTELLIGENCE AND FACTS WERE BEING FIXED AROUND THE POLICY."

AFTER THE DISCLOSURE, MICHIGAN CONGRESSMAN JOHN CONYERS WROTE TO PRESIDENT BUSH ON BEHALF OF 89 HOUSE DEMOCRATS, SAYING THAT IF THIS WAS TRUE...

...IT RAISES TROUBLING NEW QUESTIONS REGARDING THE LEGAL JUSTIFICATIONS FOR THE WAR AS WELL AS THE INTEGRITY OF YOUR OWN ADMINISTRATION.

THE BRITISH MEMO CREATED A NEW ASSESSMENT OF WHAT HAD TAKEN PLACE IN THE DAYS LEADING TO AMERICA'S INVASION OF IRAQ IN MARCH 2003. THE FOLLOWING IS A PARTIAL CHRONOLOGY...

ON NOVEMBER 21, 2001, PRESIDENT BUSH WAS REPORTED TO HAVE INSTRUCTED DEFENSE SECRETARY RUMSFELD TO REVIEW WHAT MIGHT BE NEEDED TO OUST SADDAM HUSSEIN.

THE #1 NEW YORK TIMES BESTSELLER

"*Against All Enemies* is too good to be ignored... It is a rarity among Washington insider memoirs—it's a thumping good read."
—*The New York Times Book Review*

Against All Enemies

Inside America's War on Terror

With a New Foreword by the Author

Richard A. Clarke

WORLD NEWS

U.S. CONSIDERS MOVING AGAINST SADDAM

BY JULY 2002, THERE WERE NEWSPAPER ACCOUNTS DETAILING WHAT ACTIONS WERE BEING CONSIDERED.

The PRICE of LOYALTY

George W. Bush, the White House, and the Education of Paul O'Neill

RON SUSKIND
WINNER OF THE PULITZER PRIZE

BOOKS BY THE ADMINISTRATION'S FORMER COUNTERTERRORISM ADVISER RICHARD CLARKE AND FORMER TREASURY SECRETARY PAUL O'NEILL CLAIMED THAT THE PRESIDENT HAD DECIDED TO INVADE IRAQ IN THE SUMMER OF 2002.

VETERANS OF FOREIGN WARS OF THE UNITED STATES

ON AUGUST 26, 2002, VICE PRESIDENT CHENEY, SPEAKING BEFORE THE VFW, DECLARED...

...THERE IS NO DOUBT THAT SADDAM HUSSEIN NOW HAS WEAPONS OF MASS DESTRUCTION.

THERE IS NO DOUBT THAT HE IS AMASSING THEM TO USE AGAINST OUR FRIENDS, OUR ALLIES, AND AGAINST US.

ON OCTOBER 16, 2002, CONGRESS VOTED TO AUTHORIZE OUR GOING TO WAR IN IRAQ.

ON FEBRUARY 5, 2003, SECRETARY OF STATE POWELL PRESENTED AMERICA'S REASONS FOR GOING TO WAR TO THE UN SECURITY COUNCIL. THEY RELIED HEAVILY ON AMERICAN CLAIMS FOR THE EXISTENCE OF IRAQI WEAPONS OF MASS DESTRUCTION AND SUPPORT OF TERRORISM; BOTH CLAIMS WERE LATER DISCREDITED.

PRESIDENT BUSH STATED THAT HE DID NOT DECIDE TO INVADE IRAQ UNTIL AFTER POWELL'S SPEECH.

DEADLY VIOLENCE BY INSURGENTS CONTINUED IN NORTHERN AND CENTRAL IRAQ THROUGH THE FIRST WEEK IN JUNE, CLIMAXING IN A MOTORCYCLE SUICIDE BOMBING AND THREE CAR BOMBINGS ON JUNE 2 AND THREE MORE ON JUNE 7.

MORE THAN 97 PEOPLE HAD BEEN KILLED AND 180 WOUNDED IN ATTACKS SINCE MAY 23.

IN EARLY JUNE, THE 9/11 COMMISSION MEMBERS, WHO ISSUED THEIR REPORT A YEAR EARLIER, CAME TOGETHER UNDER PRIVATE FUNDING IN AN ATTEMPT TO ASCERTAIN ON WHICH OF ITS RECOMMENDATIONS THE GOVERNMENT HAD ACTED.

ON DECEMBER 5, 2005, THE COMMISSION ISSUED A REPORT CARD RATING THE ACTIONS OF CONGRESS ON THESE MEASURES.
THE VERDICT WAS ESSENTIALLY A FAILURE. "THE RESULTS WERE DISMAL," SAID FORMER GOVERNOR THOMPSON.

ON JUNE 8, IRAQ'S SHIITE AND KURDISH LEADERS ANNOUNCED SUPPORT OF ETHNIC AND SECTARIAN MILITIAS, IN STARK OPPOSITION TO AMERICAN WISHES THAT THEY BE DISBANDED.

THIS SURPRISING NEWS WAS DELIVERED BY PRIME MINISTER JAAFARI, A SHIITE, AND PRESIDENT TALABANI, A KURD.

IN A REPORT MADE PUBLIC ON JUNE 9, THE JUSTICE DEPARTMENT'S INSPECTOR GENERAL GLENN A. FINE SAID THE FBI HAD MISSED FIVE OPPORTUNITIES TO LOCATE TWO OF THE 9/11 HIJACKERS IN SAN DIEGO MONTHS BEFORE THE ATTACKS. REPUBLICAN SENATOR CHARLES GRASSLEY COMMENTED...

... WE CAN HOPE THE FBI IS MAKING THE NEEDED CHANGES, BUT THE SIMPLE ANSWER IS IT LOOKS LIKE THEY'VE GOT A LONG WAY TO GO.

VARIOUS POLLS IN JUNE REVEALED A LOSS OF SUPPORT FOR THE WAR IN IRAQ AND A DROP IN THE PRESIDENT'S APPROVAL RATINGS.

60% FOR WITHDRAWAL OF SOME OR ALL OF TROOPS.
[GALLUP POLL]

2/3 BELIEVE THE U.S. HAS GOTTEN BOGGED DOWN IN IRAQ.
[ABC/WASHINGTON POST POLL]

42% APPROVE THE PRESIDENT'S ACTIONS.

AFTER WEEKS OF CONTENTION, ON JUNE 16, SUNNI ARABS ACCEPTED A COMPROMISE GIVING THEM GREATER INFLUENCE OVER THE DRAFTING OF AN IRAQI CONSTITUTION.
MANY HOPE THIS WILL SLOW THE INSURGENCY, HEAVILY SUPPORTED BY IRAQ'S MINORITY SUNNI COMMUNITY.

IN A NEW SHOWING OF STRENGTH, TALIBAN FORCES ATTACKED A POLICE STATION IN KANDAHAR PROVINCE ON JUNE 18, CAPTURING THE POLICE AND DISTRICT CHIEFS AS WELL AS 11 OFFICERS.

IN IRAQ, THE INSURGENT UPRISING DID NOT SLOW DOWN; ATTACKS KILLED 75 PEOPLE IN TWO DAYS.

BOMB ATTACKS BY IRAQI INSURGENTS EMPLOYING DEADLIER NEW DEVICES CAUSED MORE AMERICAN DEATHS AND DESTRUCTION IN THE PREVIOUS TWO MONTHS THAN DURING ANY SIMILAR PERIOD BEFORE.
IN MAY 2005 THERE WERE 700+ ATTACKS USING IMPROVISED EXPLOSIVE DEVICES (IED'S), THE MOST SINCE THE 2003 AMERICAN INVASION.
33 AMERICANS WERE KILLED IN MAY BY IEDS AND 35 BY MID-JUNE.

IN CONTRAST TO VICE PRESIDENT CHENEY'S MAY 31 DECLARATION THAT THE IRAQI INSURGENCY WAS IN ITS "LAST THROES," GEN. GEORGE P. ABIZAID TOLD THE SENATE ARMED SERVICES COMMITTEE ON JUNE 23 THAT THE ENEMY'S...

...OVERALL STRENGTH IS ABOUT THE SAME.

THERE'S A LOT OF WORK TO BE DONE AGAINST THE INSURGENCY.

IN A SURPRISING DEVELOPMENT, MAHMOUD AHMADINEJAD, OBSCURE BUT FOR HIS HARD-LINE ANTIREFORM, ANTI-WEST, AND ANTI-ISRAEL POSITIONS, IS ELECTED IRAN'S PRESIDENT IN A LANDSLIDE IN LATE JUNE.
HE CALLS FOR UNITY AND A STRONG ISLAMIC NATION.

ON JUNE 26, FOUR SUICIDE BOMB ATTACKS BY IRAQI INSURGENTS AGAINST IRAQI POLICE AND ARMED FORCES IN MOSUL KILLED 38 AND WOUNDED DOZENS MORE.

BOTH DEFENSE SECRETARY RUMSFELD AND GEN. ABIZAID NOW SUGGEST THAT THIS INSURGENCY COULD LAST A DOZEN YEARS.

IN A PREPARED SPEECH ON JUNE 28, PRESIDENT BUSH DECLARED THAT THE SACRIFICE OF AMERICAN LIVES...

...IS WORTH IT AND IS VITAL TO THE FUTURE SECURITY OF OUR COUNTRY.

IN RESPONSE TO FINDINGS OF THE SILBERMAN-ROBB COMMISSION, WHICH EVALUATED THE INTELLIGENCE AGENCIES' ABILITY TO EVALUATE THREATS OF WMD, PRESIDENT BUSH CREATED A NEW FBI DIVISION ON JUNE 29 THAT ERODED THE BOUNDARIES BETWEEN FOREIGN AND DOMESTIC INTELLIGENCE ACTIVITIES.

THIS SEEMINGLY CONSOLIDATED THE POWERS OF NEWLY APPOINTED INTELLIGENCE DIRECTOR JOHN NEGROPONTE.

TALIBAN ACTIVITY GREW MORE BRAZEN AND THREATENING IN AFGHANISTAN IN JUNE, WITH KIDNAPPINGS, VARIOUS ACTS OF VIOLENCE, AND THE DOWNING OF AN AMERICAN HELICOPTER.

WHRAM!

ON JULY 6, *NEW YORK TIMES* REPORTER JUDITH MILLER IS SENTENCED TO JAIL FOR REFUSING TO GIVE THE NAME OF HER CONFIDENTIAL SOURCE IDENTIFYING VALERIE PLAME WILSON AS A CIA AGENT

TERRORIST BOMBS EXPLODED ALMOST SIMULTANEOUSLY INSIDE THREE LONDON SUBWAY TRAINS AND A DOUBLE-DECKER BUS ON JULY 7, KILLING AT LEAST 56 PEOPLE AND INJURING MORE THAN 700.
A GROUP CLAIMING TO BE ALLIED WITH AL QAEDA CLAIMED RESPONSIBILITY FOR THE ATTACKS.

ON JULY 12, BRITISH POLICE SAID A GROUP OF BRITISH-BORN MEN, IDENTIFIED BY CLOSED-CIRCUIT CAMERAS, WAS RESPONSIBLE FOR THE ATTACKS. THE BODY OF ONE TERRORIST HAD ALREADY BEEN FOUND IN THE WRECKAGE.
PROPERTY BELONGING TO OTHERS WAS ALSO DISCOVERED.

IN MID-JULY, IRAQI INTERIOR MINISTER BAYAN JABR DISCLOSED THAT 8,175 IRAQIS HAD BEEN KILLED BY INSURGENTS IN THE TEN MONTHS ENDING MAY 31, FOR AN AVERAGE OF 817 PER MONTH. IN JUNE, JABR HAD SAID THAT 12,000 IRAQIS HAD BEEN KILLED BY INSURGENTS IN THE 24 MONTHS SINCE THE U.S. INVASION, OR AN AVERAGE OF 500 PER MONTH. HOWEVER, THE BRITISH MEDICAL JOURNAL *THE LANCET* LATER ESTIMATED THAT 600,000 IRAQIS HAD BEEN KILLED FROM MARCH 2003 TO JUNE 2006, FOR AN AVERAGE OF ABOUT 15,000 PER MONTH.

ESTIMATE BY JABR, FROM JUNE '02 TO JUNE '04.

ESTIMATE BY JABR, FROM AUGUST '04 TO MAY '05.

ESTIMATE BY *THE LANCET*, FROM MARCH '03 TO JUNE '06.

ONE CASKET = 100 KILLED

JUST TWO WEEKS AFTER THE LONDON SUBWAY AND BUS BOMBINGS, A SECOND ATTEMPT WAS MADE ON THREE LONDON SUBWAY TRAINS AND A DOUBLE-DECKER BUS; THE BOMBS FAILED TO GO OFF.

NEW YORK CITY POLICE INITIATED RANDOM CHECKS OF BACKPACKS AND PACKAGES CARRIED ONTO SUBWAY TRAINS.

BY LATE JULY, THE ADMINISTRATION WAS SPEAKING LESS OF A "WAR ON TERROR." SECRETARY RUMSFELD'S REFERENCE TO A "GLOBAL STRUGGLE AGAINST VIOLENT EXTREMISM" REFLECTED THE NEW APPROACH. AS CHAIRMAN OF THE JOINT CHIEFS OF STAFF GEN. RICHARD B. MYERS STATED, HE HAD...

...OBJECTED TO THE USE OF THE TERM "WAR ON TERRORISM" BECAUSE IF YOU CALL IT A WAR, THEN YOU THINK OF PEOPLE IN UNIFORM BEING THE SOLUTION.

IN NASA'S FIRST EFFORT SINCE THE FATAL *COLUMBIA* DISASTER IN 2003, SPACE SHUTTLE *DISCOVERY* SUCCESSFULLY LIFTS OFF ON THE MORNING OF JULY 26 WITH SEVEN ASTRONAUTS ABOARD. THIS IS AN ATTEMPT TO RESUPPLY THE INTERNATIONAL SPACE STATION.

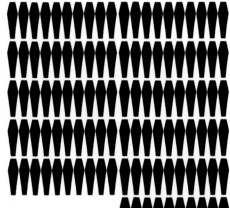

ON AUGUST 8, PENNSYLVANIA CONGRESSMAN CURT WELDON DISCLOSED THAT MORE THAN A YEAR BEFORE THE 9/11 ATTACKS, LEAD HIJACKER MOHAMED ATTA AND THREE OTHER 9/11 TERRORISTS WERE IDENTIFIED AS MEMBERS OF AN AL QAEDA CELL IN THE U.S.

AT THAT TIME, AN INTELLIGENCE UNIT CALLED ABLE DANGER PRESENTED ITS FINDINGS TO THE MILITARY'S SPECIAL OPERATIONS COMMAND AND SUGGESTED THE INFORMATION BE SHARED WITH THE FBI.
THE REQUEST WAS TURNED DOWN.

ON AUGUST 9, THE *DISCOVERY* SHUTTLE LANDS BACK ON EARTH IN THE MOJAVE DESERT, SUCCESSFULLY COMPLETING ITS MISSION COVERING 14 DAYS AND 5.8 MILLION MILES.

ON AUGUST 17, THREE CAR BOMBS EXPLODED IN A CROWDED BUS STATION IN BAGHDAD, THE MOST DISASTROUS ATTACK IN IRAQ IN ALMOST A MONTH.
APPARENTLY AIMED AT SHIITES, THE BOMB KILLED 43 IRAQIS AND INJURED 88.

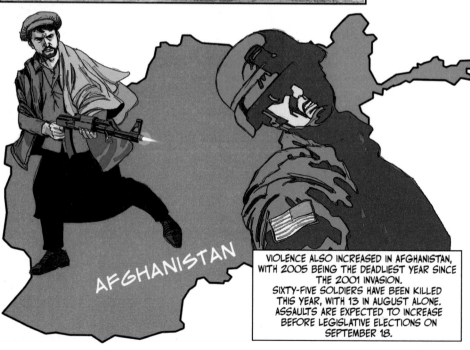

AFGHANISTAN

VIOLENCE ALSO INCREASED IN AFGHANISTAN, WITH 2005 BEING THE DEADLIEST YEAR SINCE THE 2001 INVASION.
SIXTY-FIVE SOLDIERS HAVE BEEN KILLED THIS YEAR, WITH 13 IN AUGUST ALONE.
ASSAULTS ARE EXPECTED TO INCREASE BEFORE LEGISLATIVE ELECTIONS ON SEPTEMBER 18.

ADDRESSING THOUSANDS OF NATIONAL
GUARD MEMBERS AND THEIR FAMILIES
ON AUGUST 24, PRESIDENT BUSH
DECLARED THAT IMMEDIATE WITHDRAWAL
OF U.S. TROOPS WOULD "EMBOLDEN
THE TERRORISTS" AND MAKE US MORE
VULNERABLE TO ATTACK.
HE WENT ON TO SAY...

...AS LONG AS I'M
PRESIDENT, WE WILL
STAY, WE WILL FIGHT,
AND WE WILL WIN
THE WAR!

HURRICANE KATRINA, ONE OF THE MOST DESTRUCTIVE
STORMS IN AMERICAN HISTORY, TORE INTO LOUISIANA,
MISSISSIPPI, AND ALABAMA ON AUGUST 7
WITH 145 MPH WINDS. MORE THAN A MILLION PEOPLE
WERE LEFT WITHOUT POWER. HIGHWAYS WERE SUBMERGED.
THE MOST DEVASTATING LOSSES OCCURRED IN
NEW ORLEANS, AS HUNDREDS OF THOUSANDS WERE
STRANDED IN A VIRTUALLY UNINHABITABLE CITY,
AND TENS OF THOUSANDS MORE EVACUATED TO
NEARBY STATES.
BREAKS IN TWO OF THE CITY'S LEVEES LEFT
NEIGHBORHOODS AND HOMES UNDER SEVERAL
FEET OF WATER.
EARLY DAMAGE ESTIMATES OF $25 BILLION
JUMPED TO MORE THAN $100 BILLION.

RELIEF ATTEMPTS BY FEMA AND OTHER FEDERAL AGENCIES PROVED INADEQUATE AND WERE
FIERCELY CRITICIZED. "IT REALLY MAKES US LOOK VERY MUCH LIKE BANGLADESH OR
BAGHDAD," DECLARED DAVID HERBERT DONALD, HARVARD HISTORIAN AND NATIVE
MISSISSIPPIAN, ON SEPTEMBER 2.
OTHERS SUGGESTED THAT THE RELIEF WAS LATE AND INADEQUATE BECAUSE THE PEOPLE
MOST AFFECTED WERE PREDOMINANTLY POOR AND BLACK.
MICHAEL BROWN, HEAD OF FEMA, WAS REMOVED FROM OFFICE ON SEPTEMBER 9 AND
REPLACED BY VICE ADMIRAL THAD W. ALLEN.

ALMOST A THOUSAND IRAQIS WERE KILLED AND HUNDREDS
INJURED ON AUGUST 31, IN A FRANTIC STAMPEDE OVER
A BRIDGE IN NORTHERN BAGHDAD.
INSURGENTS HAD FIRED ROCKETS AND MORTARS NEAR A
SHIITE SHRINE, TERRIFYING PILGRIMS AND CAUSING THEM TO PANIC.
SOME WERE CRUSHED AND SUFFOCATED, WHILE OTHERS, PUSHED
OFF THE BRIDGE, DROWNED IN THE TIGRIS RIVER BELOW.

ON SEPTEMBER 10, ONE DAY BEFORE THE ANNIVERSARY OF THE TRAGIC
ATTACK, THOUSANDS OF U.S. AND IRAQI TROOPS ATTACKED
TAL AFAR, A NORTHERN STRONGHOLD OF THE INSURGENCY.

IN THIS, THE LARGEST IRAQI OPERATION IN MONTHS, 11,000 SOLDIERS,
BACKED BY ROCKET-FIRING HELICOPTERS, TANKS, AND ARMORED
VEHICLES, KILLED 141 OF THE ENEMY AND CAPTURED 197; 5 IRAQI
SOLDIERS WERE KILLED AND 3 WOUNDED.

JUST DAYS BEFORE, ON SEPTEMBER 3, CHIEF JUSTICE WILLAM H. REHNQUIST
DIED OF THYROID CANCER AFTER A YEARLONG BATTLE. WITH JUSTICE SANDRA
DAY O'CONNOR DUE TO RETIRE, PRESIDENT BUSH NOMINATED TWO
JUSTICES IN QUICK SUCCESSION.

IN MID-SEPTEMBER, A DEADLY SERIES OF SUICIDE BOMBINGS ERUPTED IN IRAQ, MAINLY IN THE BAGHDAD AREA. ON SEPTEMBER 13, 80 WERE KILLED AND 160 WOUNDED BY A CAR BOMBER IN BAGHDAD. ALMOST 150 WERE KILLED AND 500 WOUNDED IN A DOZEN BOMBINGS IN THE CITY ONE DAY LATER.

AT LEAST 25 WERE KILLED BY BOMBINGS ON SEPTEMBER 16.

A CAR BOMB ON THE CAPITAL'S OUTSKIRTS CLAIMED 30 MORE THE NEXT DAY. THE HORRIFIC TOTAL CAME TO ALMOST 300 CIVILIANS KILLED AND MORE THAN DOUBLE THAT NUMBER WOUNDED IN A MERE FIVE DAYS.

IN AFGHANISTAN'S FIRST FREE LEGISLATIVE ELECTION IN 25 YEARS, MORE THAN 6 MILLION REGISTERED VOTERS DEFIED TALIBAN THREATS AND VOTED ON SEPTEMBER 13.

ON SEPTEMBER 22, SAUDI FOREIGN MINISTER PRINCE SAUD AL-FAISAL SAID HE HAD WARNED THE BUSH ADMINISTRATION THAT IRAQ WAS DISINTEGRATING. HE WENT ON...

THERE IS NO DYNAMIC NOW PULLING THE NATION TOGETHER. ALL THE DYNAMICS ARE PULLING THE NATION APART.

THREE MEMBERS OF THE ELITE 82ND AIRBORNE INFORMED HUMAN RIGHTS WATCH IN LATE SEPTEMBER THAT MEMBERS OF THEIR BATTALION SYSTEMATICALLY BEAT AND ABUSED PRISONERS TO GAIN INTELLIGENCE.

PRISONERS WERE ALLEGEDLY BEATEN, EXPOSED TO EXTREMES OF HEAT AND COLD, STACKED IN HUMAN PYRAMIDS, AND DEPRIVED OF SLEEP.

THREE BOMB-PACKED PICKUP TRUCKS WERE DETONATED BY INSURGENTS IN A TOWN NORTH OF BAGHDAD ON SEPTEMBER 29, KILLING MORE THAN 62 AND WOUNDING MANY MORE. MOST CASUALTIES WERE SHIITE CIVILIANS. AT THE SAME TIME, DEFENSE SECRETARY DONALD RUMSFELD, SPEAKING ABOUT THE INSURGENCY TO CONGRESS, DECLARED...

INSURGENCIES ULTIMATELY ARE DEFEATED BY THE INDIGENOUS PEOPLE IN THAT COUNTRY, NOT BY OUTSIDE FORCES...

...WHO CAN IN FACT CONTRIBUTE TO THE GROWTH OF AN INSURGENCY IF THEY ARE SEEN AS AN OCCUPATION FORCE.

SPEAKING BEFORE THE NATIONAL ENDOWMENT FOR DEMOCRACY ON OCTOBER 6, PRESIDENT BUSH STATED THAT THE U.S. AND ITS ALLIES HAD FOILED 10 SERIOUS TERRORIST PLOTS SINCE SEPTEMBER 11.
THIS INCLUDED ONE IN 2002 TO USE HIJACKED PLANES TO TARGET WEST COAST TARGETS AS WELL AS A SIMILAR PLAN IN 2003 TO HIT THE EAST COAST. HE ALSO SAID...

THE UNITED STATES MAKES NO DISTINCTION BETWEEN THOSE WHO COMMIT ACTS OF TERROR AND THOSE WHO SUPPORT AND HARBOR THEM.

A PENTAGON REPORT MADE PUBLIC ON OCTOBER 13 STATED THAT IRAQI SECURITY FORCES HAVE BEEN SHOWING "STEADY PROGRESS" IN THEIR CAPABILITIES. HOWEVER, AN UNNAMED OFFICER IN IRAQ DECLARED...

THE IRAQI ARMY WILL NOT BE READY FOR CONTINUOUS OPERATIONS FOR AT LEAST ANOTHER YEAR.

[AT PRESENT] WE CAN COMPENSATE FOR THEIR LACK OF CAPABILITY IN CRITICAL AREAS.

AS VOTES FOR IRAQ'S NEW CONSTITUTION WERE BEING TABULATED IN MID-OCTOBER, VOICES OF DISCONTENT WERE BEING HEARD MORE FREQUENTLY. KENNETH POLLACK, FORMER CIA ANALYST, STATED...

"THEIR [THE BUSH ADMINISTRATION] WHOLE THEORY ABOUT HOW THIS IS GOING TO WORK OUT ISN'T WORKING."

"THE THEORY THAT DEMOCRACY IS THE ANTIDOTE TO INSURGENCY GETS DISPROVED ON THE GROUND EVERY DAY."

ON OCTOBER 20, LAURENCE WILKERSON, FORMER CHIEF OF STAFF TO SECRETARY OF STATE POWELL, DECLARED THAT THE NATION'S FOREIGN POLICY HAD BEEN TAKEN OVER BY A "CHENEY-RUMSFELD CABAL." SPEAKING BEFORE THE NEW AMERICA FOUNDATION, HE SAID...

[PRESIDENT BUSH] IS NOT VERSED IN INTERNATIONAL RELATIONS AND NOT MUCH INTERESTED IN THEM, EITHER.

ELECTION OFFICIALS IN IRAQ REPORTED ON OCTOBER 25 THAT THE NEW CONSTITUTION HAD BEEN APPROVED BY 79% OF THE VOTERS AND PARLIAMENTARY ELECTIONS WOULD BE HELD IN DECEMBER.

VOTING WAS STRONGLY DIVIDED ALONG SECTARIAN LINES. THREE PRIMARILY SUNNI PROVINCES VOTED AGAINST APPROVAL, FALLING JUST SHORT OF DEFEATING IT.

I. LEWIS [SCOOTER] LIBBY JR., VICE PRESIDENT CHENEY'S CHIEF OF STAFF, IS INDICTED BY A FEDERAL GRAND JURY ON OCTOBER 28 ON FIVE FELONY CHARGES ARISING FROM THE VALERIE PLAME WILSON CASE. "WE DIDN'T GET THE STRAIGHT STORY," DECLARED PROSECUTOR PATRICK J. FITZGERALD, "AND WE HAD TO TAKE ACTION."

AT LEAST 57 DIE AND MORE THAN 100 ARE WOUNDED ON NOVEMBER 9 IN COORDINATED TERRORIST ATTACKS ON THREE HOTELS IN AMMAN, JORDAN. THE MOST DEVASTATION OCCURS AT A WEDDING PARTY. ABU MUSAB AL-ZARQAWI, CHIEF OF SO-CALLED AL QAEDA IN MESOPOTAMIA, IS SUSPECTED TO HAVE PLANNED THE ATTACKS.

ON NOVEMBER 17, PENNSYLVANIA CONGRESSMAN JOHN P. MURTHA, INFLUENTIAL PROWAR DEMOCRAT, STUNNED CAPITOL HILL BY CALLING FOR IMMEDIATE WITHDRAWAL OF U.S. TROOPS IN IRAQ. ASKING THAT THEY BE WITHDRAWN WITHIN SIX MONTHS, HE SAID...

OUR MILITARY HAS DONE EVERYTHING THAT HAS BEEN ASKED OF THEM. IT IS TIME TO BRING THEM HOME.

ON NOVEMBER 21, AT AN ARAB-LEAGUE-SPONSORED RECONCILIATION CONFERENCE IN CAIRO, EGYPT, 100 SUNNI, SHIITE, AND KURDISH IRAQI LEADERS DEMANDED "A WITHDRAWAL OF FOREIGN TROOPS ON A SPECIFIED TIMETABLE DEPENDENT ON AN IMMEDIATE NATIONAL PROGRAM FOR REBUILDING NATIONAL FORCES."
IRAQI INTERIOR MINISTER BAYAN JABR COMMENTED, "BY MID-NEXT YEAR, WE WILL BE 75% DONE IN BUILDING OUR FORCE, AND BY THE END OF NEXT YEAR, IT WILL BE FULLY READY."

TWO DAYS LATER, PENTAGON OFFICIALS CLAIMED THAT IF SECURITY CONDITIONS IMPROVED, THERE WOULD BE REDUCTIONS IN TROOP LEVELS BY LATE NEXT YEAR.
SECRETARY OF STATE CONDOLEEZA RICE SAID...

HOWEVER, ON NOVEMBER 30, IN A SPEECH AT THE NAVAL ACADEMY, PRESIDENT BUSH CALLED FOR "TIME AND PATIENCE" AND REFUTED "ARTIFICIAL TIMETABLES SET BY POLITICIANS."

PULLING OUT OUR TROOPS BEFORE THEY'VE ACHIEVED THEIR PURPOSE IS NOT A PLAN FOR VICTORY.

"I SUSPECT THAT AMERICAN FORCES ARE NOT GOING TO BE NEEDED IN THE NUMBERS THEY ARE FOR THAT MUCH LONGER."

IN IRAQ, MILITARY ACTION AND BLOODSHED CONTINUED IN EARLY DECEMBER. A BOMB KILLED 10 AND WOUNDED 11 U.S. MARINES WHO WERE ON FOOT PATROL IN BAGHDAD, AND TWO SUICIDE BOMBERS KILLED 36 AND WOUNDED 72 AT THE CAPITAL'S MAIN POLICE ACADEMY.

A NEW YORK TIMES/CBS POLL RELEASED DECEMBER 8 REVEALED THAT PRESIDENT BUSH'S APPROVAL RATING HAD IMPROVED SUBSTANTIALLY THAT MONTH; A PERCEIVED IMPROVING ECONOMY WAS BELIEVED TO BE THE REASON.

35%	40%		
NOV.	DEC.		PRESIDENT'S APPROVAL RATING

57%	53%	
NOV.	DEC.	PRESIDENT'S JOB DISAPPROVAL RATING

47%	56%	
NOV.	DEC.	BELIEVE NATIONAL ECONOMY IS GOOD

IN EARLY DECEMBER, CURRENT AND FORMER U.S. OFFICIALS DISCLOSED THAT A CLAIMED IRAQ-AL QAEDA LINK USED TO JUSTIFY THE IRAQ WAR WAS A LIE INDUCED BY THE THREAT OF EGYPTIAN TORTURE.

IBN AL-SHAYKH AL-LIBI, A HIGH-RANKING AL QAEDA LEADER IN U.S. CUSTODY, WAS TURNED OVER TO EGYPT FOR INTERROGATION AND LIED TO ESCAPE FURTHER HARM.

NO... NO... I TALK... I TALK.

ON DECEMBER 15, MILLIONS OF IRAQIS TURNED OUT TO VOTE FOR PARLIAMENT MEMBERS TO SERVE FOUR-YEAR TERMS. AN ESTIMATED 70% OF ELIGIBLE VOTERS WENT TO THE POLLS. PRESIDENT BUSH CALLED THE TURNOUT "A MAJOR STEP FORWARD."
SPEAKING FROM THE OVAL OFFICE ON DECEMBER 19, PRESIDENT BUSH ASKED THE NATION "NOT TO GIVE IN TO DESPAIR" OVER THE IRAQ WAR AND HINTED AT TROOP WITHDRAWALS IN 2006. HE WENT ON...

WE WILL SEE THE IRAQI MILITARY GAINING STRENGTH AND CONFIDENCE AND THE DEMOCRATIC PROCESS MOVING FORWARD. AS THESE ACHIEVEMENTS COME, IT SHOULD REQUIRE FEWER AMERICAN TROOPS TO ACCOMPLISH OUR MISSION.

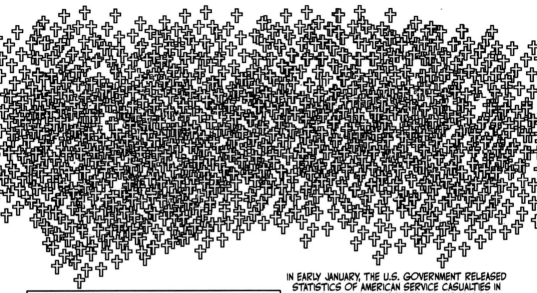

IN EARLY JANUARY, THE U.S. GOVERNMENT RELEASED STATISTICS OF AMERICAN SERVICE CASUALTIES IN IRAQ SINCE THE WAR STARTED IN MARCH 2003.

IT NOTED THAT 844 AMERICAN SERVICEMEN AND WOMEN HAD BEEN KILLED IN 2005 COMPARED TO 848 IN 2004; 5,557 HAD BEEN WOUNDED THROUGH DECEMBER 3 OF 2005, COMPARED TO 7,989 IN 2004; AND 427 OF THE MILITARY DEATHS IN 2005, OR MORE THAN 50% OF THE TOTAL, WERE DUE TO HOMEMADE BOMBS CALLED IED'S.

IN TOTAL, AMERICA HAD SUFFERED 2,178 MILITARY DEATHS SINCE THE WAR BEGAN, AND 15,955 WOUNDED. A SEPARATE SURVEY, BY IRAQI BODY COUNT, ESTIMATED IRAQI MILITARY DEATHS AT MORE THAN 30,000 SINCE THE START OF THE WAR.

PROMINENT REPUBLICAN LOBBYIST JACK ABRAMOFF PLEADED GUILTY ON JANUARY 3 TO THREE FELONY COUNTS AS PART SETTLEMENT FOR HIS ROLE IN A MAJOR WASHINGTON CORRUPTION SCANDAL.
IN EXCHANGE FOR AGREEING TO HELP THE PROSECUTION, HE WAS GIVEN A REDUCED PRISON SENTENCE OF TEN YEARS AND MUST PAY MORE THAN $26 MILLION IN TAX PENALTIES AND RESTITUTION.

A RASH OF DEADLY INSURGENT ATTACKS IN BAGHDAD, KARBALA, RAMADI, MIQDADIYA, AND OTHER AREAS WERE UNLEASHED IN EARLY AND MID-JANUARY, JUST WEEKS AFTER THE PARLIAMENTARY ELECTIONS OF DECEMBER 15. MORE THAN 260 IRAQIS WERE KILLED AND AS MANY WOUNDED.

ON JANUARY 30, MOWAFFAK AL-RUBAIE, CHAIRMAN OF THE IRAQI GROUP PLANNING THE TRANSFER OF SECURITY FORCES FROM THE AMERICANS TO THE IRAQIS, DECLARED THAT THE FOREIGN TROOP CONTINGENT WOULD PROBABLY DROP UNDER 100,000 BY YEAR'S END.
HE ADDED... "BY THE END OF 2007, THE OVERWHELMING MAJORITY OF THE MULTINATIONAL FORCES WILL HAVE LEFT THE COUNTRY."

TRYING TO DECREASE THE DEADLY TOLL OF IED'S ON AMERICAN FORCES, THE PENTAGON DECIDED IN EARLY FEBRUARY TO SPEND $3.5 BILLION, TRIPLING THE PREVIOUS BUDGET, ON ITS PROGRAM TO CONFRONT THIS THREAT. DIRECTOR OF NATIONAL INTELLIGENCE JOHN NEGROPONTE SAID THESE DEVICES...

...REMAIN THE MOST SIGNIFICANT DAY-TO-DAY THREAT TO COALITION FORCES AND A COMPLEX CHALLENGE FOR THE INTELLIGENCE COMMUNITY.

PAUL R. PILLAR, A CIA OFFICIAL WHO SUPERVISED ASSESSMENTS CONCERNING THE MIDDLE EAST FROM 2000 TO 2005, SAID THE BUSH ADMINISTRATION DISREGARDED PREWAR EVIDENCE TO JUSTIFY ITS GOING TO WAR WITH IRAQ.

"IF THE ENTIRE BODY OF OFFICIAL INTELLIGENCE IN IRAQ HAD A POLICY IMPLICATION, IT WAS TO AVOID WAR, OR IF WAR WAS GOING TO BE LAUNCHED, TO PREPARE FOR A MESSY AFTERMATH. WHAT IS MOST REMARKABLE ABOUT PREWAR INTELLIGENCE...IS THAT IT PLAYED SO SMALL A ROLE IN ONE OF THE MOST IMPORTANT U.S. POLICY DECISIONS IN DECADES...INTELLIGENCE WAS MISUSED PUBLICLY TO JUSTIFY DECISIONS THAT HAD ALREADY BEEN MADE..."
PILLAR ALSO RECOMMENDED THE CREATION OF AN INDEPENDENT OFFICE TO ASSESS THE USE OF INTELLIGENCE.

ON FEBRUARY 11, VICE PRESIDENT DICK CHENEY ACCIDENTALLY SHOT AND WOUNDED PROMINENT TEXAS LAWYER HARRY M. WHITTINGTON WHILE QUAIL HUNTING IN SOUTHERN TEXAS. THE VICE PRESIDENT DELAYED RELEASING THE NEWS FOR A DAY.

ARRESTS AND INTERROGATION OF TERRORISTS IN AFGHANISTAN IN MID-FEBRUARY REVEALED THAT THEIR ATTEMPTED ATTACKS HAD BEEN ORGANIZED IN PAKISTAN BY OUSTED MEMBERS OF THE TALIBAN AND WITH LITTLE PAKISTANI GOVERNMENT INTERFERENCE.

IN PERHAPS THE WORST SECTARIAN VIOLENCE SINCE THE START OF THE WAR, AT LEAST 138 PEOPLE WERE KILLED IN THE TWO DAYS FOLLOWING THE FEBRUARY 22, 2006, BOMBING OF THE IMPORTANT ASKARIYA SHRINE IN SAMARRA.

THE MOST POWERFUL SUNNI GROUP IN THE IRAQI PARLIAMENT SUSPENDED TALKS ABOUT FORMING A GOVERNMENT, AND THE NATION APPEARED ON THE BRINK OF OPEN CIVIL WAR.

ON FEBRUARY 24, IMAMS THROUGHOUT IRAQ CALLED FOR AN END TO THE SECTARIAN VIOLENCE THAT HAD LED TO 170 DEATHS IN THE LAST THREE DAYS.

A NATIONWIDE DAYTIME CURFEW WAS EXTENDED FOR TWO MORE DAYS.

ON THE LAST DAY OF FEBRUARY, MORE THAN 75 IRAQIS WERE KILLED AND MANY MORE WOUNDED AS INSURGENTS STRUCK THROUGHOUT IRAQ. FIVE DEADLY BOMBINGS OCCURRED IN BAGHDAD ALONE. IN ONE WEEK, 379 IRAQIS WERE KILLED AND 458 INJURED.

ON MARCH 12, VIOLENCE CONTINUED IN IRAQ AS 46 WERE KILLED AND 200 WOUNDED WHEN SIX CAR BOMBS ERUPTED IN CROWDED BAGHDAD MARKETS IN SHIITE NEIGHBORHOODS.

IN REACTION, SHIITE MILITIAS IMMEDIATELY TOOK UP ARMS.

AN ARTICLE IN *THE NEW YORK TIMES* ON MARCH 13, ALLEGED THAT IN THE OPENING WEEKS OF THE WAR, GEN. TOMMY FRANKS AND DEFENSE SECRETARY DONALD RUMSFELD, INTENT ON RACING TO BAGHDAD, DISMISSED SUGGESTIONS BY GEN. WILLIAM S. WALLACE TO DELAY THE MARCH IN ORDER TO SUPPRESS THE THREAT OF FEDAYEENS (FORMER SADDAM FIGHTERS) IN THEIR REAR. GENERAL WALLACE HAD SAID...

THE ENEMY WE'RE FIGHTING IS A BIT DIFFERENT THAN THE ONE WE WAR-GAMED AGAINST BECAUSE OF THESE PARA-MILITARY FORCES.

"WOULD THIS MEAN A LONGER WAR?" HE WAS ASKED.

IT'S BEGINNING TO LOOK THAT WAY.

GENERAL WALLACE'S SUGGESTIONS WERE NOT TAKEN.

ON MARCH 13, BRITISH DEFENSE SECRETARY JOHN REID, CITING THE PREPAREDNESS OF IRAQI FORCES, SAID HIS NATION WOULD FURTHER REDUCE ITS TROOPS IN IRAQ BY ABOUT 10% IN MAY.
FROM AN INITIAL 46,000, BRITISH TROOPS HAD DECLINED STEADILY...

DECLINE OF BRITISH FORCES

46,000 TROOPS IN 2003

18,000 TROOPS IN MAY 2004

8,000 TROOPS IN MARCH 2005

7,200 TROOPS IN MAY 2005

IN A SPEECH ON MARCH 13, PRESIDENT BUSH REAFFIRMED HIS COMMITMENT TO THE AMERICAN INVASION OF IRAQ, THOUGH HE CONCEDED THE CONFLICT HAD CAUSED UNEXPECTED PROBLEMS. HE CONTINUED...

I WISH I COULD TELL YOU THAT THE VIOLENCE IS WANING AND THAT THE ROAD AHEAD WILL BE SMOOTH...

...IT WILL NOT.

THERE WILL BE MORE TOUGH FIGHTING AND MORE DAYS OF STRUGGLE.

OVER TWO DAYS IN THE MIDDLE OF MARCH, 85 BODIES WERE FOUND IN BAGHDAD, ALL EXECUTED AND MANY VICTIMS OF TORTURE. IT WAS NOT CLEAR WHETHER THESE WERE VICTIMS OF SHIITE OR SUNNI INSURGENTS, OR POSSIBLY OF BOTH.

ON THE THIRD ANNIVERSARY OF THE IRAQI WAR ON MARCH 19-- AND NEARLY THREE YEARS SINCE PRESIDENT BUSH DECLARED "MISSION ACCOMPLISHED"--FORMER IRAQI PRIME MINISTER AYAD ALLAWI SAID, "IT IS UNFORTUNATE THAT WE ARE IN A CIVIL WAR." OTHERS, HOWEVER, DIFFERED...

GENERAL GEORGE W. CASEY JR.

"WE ARE A LONG WAY FROM CIVIL WAR. OVER 2006, WE WILL CONTINUE TO SEE A GRADUAL REDUCTION IN COALITION FORCES."

PRESIDENT GEORGE W. BUSH

"I'M ENCOURAGED BY THE PROGRESS."

DEFENSE SECRETARY DONALD RUMSFELD

THE CONTINUING SECTARIAN VIOLENCE, WHICH BEGAN ON FEBRUARY 22, WITH THE ATTACK ON A SHIITE SHRINE IN SAMARRA, INCREASINGLY LOOKED LIKE CIVIL WAR. THREE YEARS AGO, WHEN THE WAR HAD STARTED, A SHORT FIGHT WAS PREDICTED. PLANS SUGGESTED THAT MOST TROOPS WOULD BE HOME BY THE FALL OF 2003. BUT AS OF THIS ANNIVERSARY... 133,000 TROOPS WERE STILL IN IRAQ. 2,313 AMERICAN MILITARY PERSONNEL AND PENTAGON CIVILIANS HAD BEEN KILLED IN IRAQ. 1,811 KILLED IN ACTION. 7,912 MILITARY PERSONNEL HAD BEEN SEVERELY WOUNDED AND SENT HOME. 9,212 MILITARY PERSONNEL HAD BEEN WOUNDED BUT RETURNED TO ACTION.

"TURNING OUR BACKS ON POSTWAR IRAQ TODAY WOULD BE THE MODERN EQUIVALENT OF HANDING GERMANY BACK TO THE NAZIS."

...THE START DATE FOR THE MILITARY CAMPAIGN IS NOW PENCILED IN FOR MARCH 10. THIS IS WHEN THE BOMBING WILL BEGIN...

TOP SECRET

A SECOND CONFIDENTIAL MEMO WRITTEN ON JANUARY 31, 2003, BY THE CHIEF POLICY ADVISER TO BRITISH PRIME MINISTER TONY BLAIR WAS LEAKED; IT DECLARED THAT PRESIDENT BUSH HAD DETERMINED TO START THE WAR IN IRAQ ON MARCH 10 DESPITE ANY FINDINGS OR RECOMMENDATIONS BY THE UN.

PART OF DAVID MANNING'S MEMO APPEARED IN THE BOOK *LAWLESS WORLD*, PUBLISHED IN JANUARY, ON LONDON'S CHANNEL 4 IN FEBRUARY, AND IN *THE NEW YORK TIMES* IN MID-MARCH.

IN THE YEAR'S MOST VIOLENT DAY FOR AMERICANS IN IRAQ, NINE SERVICE PEOPLE WERE KILLED ON APRIL 3 IN THE INSURGENT BASTION OF ANBAR PROVINCE. FOUR WERE SLAIN BY INSURGENT ATTACKS AND FIVE DIED WHEN THEIR TRUCK ACCIDENTALLY TURNED OVER.

WITH THE IRAQI GOVERNMENT STILL UNFORMED, THREE SUICIDE BOMBERS KILL AT LEAST 71 AND WOUND 140 AT THE SHIITE BARATHA MOSQUE IN BAGHDAD.

U.S. AMBASSADOR ZALMAY KHALILZAD WARNS THAT IF A GOVERNMENT IS NOT FORMED SOON, A SECTARIAN WAR COULD ENVELOP THE ENTIRE REGION.

A 10-PAGE INTERNAL REPORT, PREPARED BY THE U.S. EMBASSY AND THE MILITARY IN IRAQ ON JANUARY 31, RATED THE STABILITY OF 6 OF IRAQ'S 18 PROVINCES AS "SERIOUS" AND ONE AS "CRITICAL."
THE REPORT CONFIRMED THAT THE HARDENING OF ETHNIC AND RELIGIOUS SCHISMS TOGETHER WITH MASS MIGRATIONS SUGGEST THAT A DE FACTO PARTITION IS TAKING PLACE.

ON APRIL 29, IRAQI VICE PRESIDENT ABDEL ABDUL MAHDI SAYS AT LEAST 100,000 IRAQIS HAVE FLED THEIR HOMES.

IN ANSWER TO WIDESPREAD CRITICISMS OF HIS DEFENSE
SECRETARY--INCLUDING THOSE VOICED BY SIX RETIRED
GENERALS--PRESIDENT BUSH STRONGLY RESTATED HIS
SUPPORT OF DONALD H. RUMSFELD.
ON APRIL 14. HE SAID...

"SECRETARY RUMSFELD'S ENERGETIC AND STEADY
LEADERSHIP IS EXACTLY WHAT IS NEEDED AT THIS
CRITICAL PERIOD."

RESPONDING TO DOMESTIC AND AMERICAN PRESSURE,
IRAQI PRIME MINISTER IBRAHIM AL-JAAFARI GAVE UP ANY
BID TO RETAIN HIS POST ON APRIL 20, REMOVING AN
IMPORTANT IMPEDIMENT TO IRAQ'S FORMING A NEW
GOVERNMENT. JAAFARI DECLARED...
"I CANNOT ACCEPT BEING A BARRICADE OR LOOKING
LIKE A BARRICADE."

ON APRIL 21 SHIITE LEADERS SELECTED NOURI AL-MALIKI
AS THEIR NOMINEE, AND ONE DAY LATER HE WAS INSTALLED
AS PRIME MINISTER.
BOTH IRAQI AND AMERICAN OFFICIALS VIEWED THIS AS
AN IMPORTANT STEP TOWARD ENDING SECTARIAN VIOLENCE.

THE UN'S INTERNATIONAL ATOMIC
ENERGY AGENCY DECLARED ON
APRIL 28 THAT IRAN HAD ENDED
ITS COOPERATION WITH NUCLEAR
INSPECTORS AND RECOMMENCED
ITS NUCLEAR ENRICHMENT
PROGRAM. PRESIDENT MAHMOUD
AHMADINEJAD SAID...
"THOSE WHO WANT TO PREVENT
IRANIANS FROM OBTAINING THEIR
RIGHT SHOULD KNOW THAT WE
DO NOT GIVE A DAMN ABOUT
SUCH RESOLUTIONS."

BUT DEADLY VIOLENCE CONTINUED IN AND AROUND BAGHDAD
ON APRIL 24. FORTY CIVILIANS AND SECURITY FORCE
RECRUITS WERE FOUND DEAD, WHILE A SERIES OF CAR BOMBS
KILLED AT LEAST 10 PEOPLE AND WOUNDED 76.

AT THE END OF APRIL, THE STATE DEPARTMENT REPORTED THAT THE NUMBER OF INSURGENT ATTACKS IN IRAQ HAD GROWN TREMENDOUSLY IN 2005.

TEN U.S. SOLDIERS ARE KILLED IN A HELICOPTER CRASH IN AFGHANISTAN ON MAY 6, AS VIOLENCE CONTINUES IN THE REGION. A BRITISH HELICOPTER, APPARENTLY HIT BY ROCKET FIRE, CRASHES ON THAT SAME DAY IN BASRA, KILLING FIVE BRITISH SERVICE PEOPLE.

CIA DIRECTOR PORTER GOSS RESIGNS HIS POST ON MAY 5, ENDING HIS TUMULTUOUS 19-MONTH TENURE. THREE DAYS LATER, PRESIDENT BUSH PICKS GEN. MICHAEL V. HAYDEN TO REPLACE HIM.

THERE WERE NEARLY 3,500 TERRORIST ATTACKS IN IRAQ (1/3 OF THE WORLD WIDE TOTAL), RESULTING IN 8,300 DEATHS (MORE THAN 50% OF THE WORLDWIDE TOTAL). THE NUMBERS WERE DOUBLE THE PREVIOUS YEAR'S.

NEW ITALIAN PRIME MINISTER ROMANO PRODI, CALLED THE WAR IN IRAQ A "GRAVE ERROR" ON MAY 18. HE ADDED...

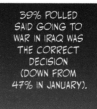

IT HAS NOT SOLVED, BUT COMPLICATED, THE SITUATION OF SECURITY. TERRORISM HAS FOUND A NEW BASE IN IRAQ AND NEW EXCUSES FOR THEIR ATTACKS BOTH INSIDE AND OUTSIDE OF THE COUNTRY.

ACCORDING TO A *NEW YORK TIMES*/CBS POLL RELEASED ON MAY 10, PRESIDENT BUSH'S APPROVAL RATINGS HAVE DROPPED TO THE LOWEST LEVELS OF HIS PRESIDENCY. SOME OF THE RESULTS WERE...

2/3 POLLED HAVE LITTLE CONFIDENCE THAT BUSH CAN END THE WAR SUCCESSFULLY.

2/3 POLLED BELIEVE THE COUNTRY IS IN WORSE SHAPE THAN WHEN BUSH TOOK OFFICE.

50% POLLED SAY DEMOCRATS COME CLOSER TO THEIR MORAL VALUES THAN REPUBLICANS.

39% POLLED SAID GOING TO WAR IN IRAQ WAS THE CORRECT DECISION (DOWN FROM 47% IN JANUARY).

THREE YEARS AFTER THE IRAQI POLICE HAD BEEN REORGANIZED, THIS ANTICIPATED CORNERSTONE OF A NEW IRAQI DEMOCRACY WAS IN SHAMBLES. SHORT OF AMERICAN ADVISERS -- THOUGH THE JUSTICE DEPARTMENT HAD SUGGESTED THOUSANDS, THE PENTAGON HAD ALLOTED A DOZEN-- THE POLICE WERE ACCUSED OF OPERATING DEATH SQUADS FOR SPECIAL INTERESTS. THEY HAVE ALSO SUFFERED A HIGH FATALITY RATE: OVER AN EQUIVALENT PERIOD OF TIME THIS YEAR, 547 POLICE WERE KILLED, OR ABOUT THE COMBINED TOTAL OF IRAQIS AND U.S. SOLDIERS KILLED.

ONE DAY AFTER NEW IRAQI PRIME MINISTER MALIKI PREDICTED THAT MOST U.S. AND BRITISH TROOPS WOULD BE GONE BY YEAR'S END, OVER 30 IRAQIS WERE KILLED ON MAY 23 BY VARIOUS ATTACKS BY INSURGENTS ACROSS THE NATION.

WHITE HOUSE SPOKESMAN TONY SNOW COUNTERED MALIKI'S REMARKS BY SAYING, "THE CONDITIONS ON THE GROUND TELL US THAT OUR JOB IS NOT DONE."

ONE WEEK LATER, PROMPTED BY REPORTS OF MARINES KILLING 24 IRAQI CIVILIANS IN HADITHA THE YEAR BEFORE, PRIME MINISTER MALIKI CONDEMNED THE AMERICAN MILITARY. HE DECLARED... "THEY CRUSH THEM (IRAQI CIVILIANS) WITH THEIR VEHICLES AND KILL THEM JUST ON SUSPICION. THIS IS COMPLETELY UNACCEPTABLE."

THE WORST AFGHAN RIOTS IN YEARS OCURRED IN KABUL ON MAY 29, SET OFF BY A DEADLY TRAFFIC ACCIDENT CAUSED BY AN AMERICAN MILITARY TRUCK.
17 AFGHANS WERE KILLED AND 250 WERE DETAINED.

IN A STEP TOWARD "NATIONAL RECONCILIATION" AND THE REINTEGRATION OF FORMER BAATH PARTY MEMBERS INTO IRAQI SOCIETY, ON JUNE 12, PRIME MINISTER MALIKI SAID HIS IRAQI GOVERNMENT WOULD RELEASE 2,500 DETAINEES, ABOUT 10% OF THOSE HELD.

ABU MUSAB AL-ZARQAWI, THE 39-YEAR-OLD ELUSIVE LEADER OF AL QAEDA IN IRAQ, WAS KILLED ON JUNE 8 WHEN A PAIR OF F-16 FIGHTERS DROPPED TWO 500-POUND BOMBS ON A HOUSE THAT INFORMANTS HAD IDENTIFIED.

PRESIDENT BUSH COMMENTED...

ZARQAWI IS DEAD, BUT...

...WE CAN EXPECT THE TERRORISTS AND INSURGENTS TO CARRY ON WITHOUT HIM.

A NEW YORK TIMES OP-ED PIECE ON JUNE 16 BY NINA KAMP, MICHAEL O'HANLON, AND AMY UNIKEWICZ REPORTED THE FOLLOWING STATISTICS...

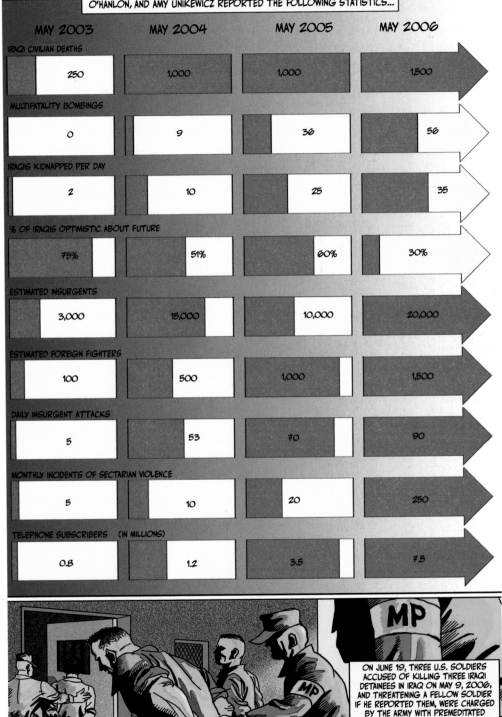

	MAY 2003	MAY 2004	MAY 2005	MAY 2006
IRAQI CIVILIAN DEATHS	250	1,000	1,000	1,500
MULTIFATALITY BOMBINGS	0	9	36	56
IRAQIS KIDNAPPED PER DAY	2	10	25	35
% OF IRAQIS OPTIMISTIC ABOUT FUTURE	75%	51%	60%	30%
ESTIMATED INSURGENTS	3,000	15,000	10,000	20,000
ESTIMATED FOREIGN FIGHTERS	100	500	1,000	1,500
DAILY INSURGENT ATTACKS	5	53	70	90
MONTHLY INCIDENTS OF SECTARIAN VIOLENCE	5	10	20	250
TELEPHONE SUBSCRIBERS (IN MILLIONS)	0.8	1.2	3.5	7.5

MP

ON JUNE 19, THREE U.S. SOLDIERS ACCUSED OF KILLING THREE IRAQI DETAINEES IN IRAQ ON MAY 9, 2006, AND THREATENING A FELLOW SOLDIER IF HE REPORTED THEM, WERE CHARGED BY THE ARMY WITH PREMEDITATED MURDER AND OBSTRUCTING JUSTICE. THE THREE WERE JAILED IN KUWAIT AWAITING HEARINGS.

I WASN'T THERE, BUT I HEARD ABOUT IT.

ANOTHER SUSPECTED KILLING IN IRAQ BECAME KNOWN ON JUNE 30, WHEN FIVE SOLDIERS WERE ACCUSED OF RAPING AN IRAQI WOMAN (IDENTIFIED AS A FIFTEEN-YEAR-OLD) AND THEN KILLING HER AND THREE FAMILY MEMBERS ON MARCH 12 NEAR THE TOWN OF MAHMUDIYA. A FELLOW SOLDIER DISCLOSED THE EVENT IN A COUNSELING SESSION.

DAYS LATER, A RECENTLY DISCHARGED GI WAS ARRESTED IN ASHEVILLE, NC, FOR BEING PART OF THE GROUP. THREE OTHERS WERE ARRESTED ON JULY 8.

DEFYING AMERICAN WARNINGS, NORTH KOREA TEST-FIRES SIX MISSILES OVER THE SEA OF JAPAN ON JULY 5; ONE MISSILE FAILS OR IS ABORTED AFTER 42 SECONDS. THE UNITED STATES "REMAINS COMMITTED TO A DIPLOMATIC SOLUTION" IN NORTH KOREA, THE WHITE HOUSE IMMEDIATELY DECLARED.

A MOB OF VIGILANTE GUNMEN SWEPT THROUGH A SUNNI DISTRICT OF BAGHDAD ON JULY 9, PULLING PEOPLE FROM HOMES AND CARS AND KILLING MORE THAN 40. THIS WAS REPORTED TO BE AN ACT OF REVENGE FOR THE BOMBING OF A SHIITE MOSQUE A DAY EARLIER. HOURS LATER, ANOTHER SHIITE MOSQUE WAS HIT, WITH 19 SLAIN.

ON JULY 12, A DAY WHEN MORE THAN 30 PEOPLE WERE KILLED IN BAGHDAD, GEN. GEORGE W. CASEY DECLARED THAT MORE U.S. TROOPS MIGHT BE NEEDED IN THE CAPITAL. PRIME MINISTER MALIKI ADDED...

WE ALL HAVE THIS LAST CHANCE TO RECONCILE AND WORK HARD TO AVOID THE CONFLICT. IF IT FAILS--GOD FORBID-- I DON'T KNOW WHAT WILL BE IRAQ'S FATE.

ACCORDING TO THE CONGRESSIONAL BUDGET OFFICE ON JULY 13, THE IRAQ WAR HAD SO FAR COST $291 BILLION. EVEN IF ALL TROOPS WERE WITHDRAWN, THE COST WAS ESTIMATED TO BE CLOSE TO $500 BILLION BY 2009.

IN CURRENT DOLLAR VALUE, THE KOREAN WAR COST $363 BILLION, THE VIETNAM WAR $346 BILLION, AND THE GULF WAR $61 BILLION.

A NEW MIDDLE EAST CONFLICT BEGAN IN MID-JULY AS THE LEBANESE GUERRILLA GROUP HEZBOLLAH, IN A SURPRISE ASSAULT, CROSSED THE ISRAELI BORDER AND KILLED EIGHT SOLDIERS WHILE CAPTURING TWO. ISRAEL RESPONDED IMMEDIATELY, IMPOSING A FULL NAVAL BLOCKADE ON LEBANON AND BOMBING BEIRUT HARBOR.

LEBANON RESPONDED, LAUNCHING MORE THAN 120 ROCKETS INTO ISRAEL, KILLING TWO AND SENDING THOUSANDS INTO BOMB SHELTERS.

THE EUROPEAN UNION CRITICIZED ISRAEL FOR "THE DISPROPORTIONATE USE OF FORCE" IN ITS RESPONSE. THE BUSH ADMINISTRATION GAVE ISRAEL TACIT APPROVAL. SECRETARY OF STATE CONDOLEEZZA RICE STATED... "ISRAEL HAS THE RIGHT TO DEFEND ITSELF. WE WOULD EXPECT NOTHING ELSE."

THE UN REPORTED ON JULY 18 THAT DEATHS OF CIVILIANS IN IRAQ AVERAGED MORE THAN 100 PER DAY IN JUNE, THE HIGHEST MONTHLY TOTAL SINCE BAGHDAD'S FALL AND TWICE THAT OF THE PREVIOUS MONTH.

THIS CAME ONE DAY AFTER GUNMEN SWEPT THROUGH A SHIITE MARKET NEAR BAGHDAD, KILLING AT LEAST 48 AND WOUNDING SCORES MORE.

IRAQ WAR

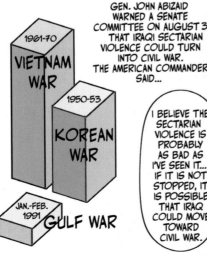

1961-70 VIETNAM WAR

1950-53 KOREAN WAR

JAN.-FEB. 1991 GULF WAR

GEN. JOHN ABIZAID WARNED A SENATE COMMITTEE ON AUGUST 3 THAT IRAQI SECTARIAN VIOLENCE COULD TURN INTO CIVIL WAR. THE AMERICAN COMMANDER SAID...

I BELIEVE THE SECTARIAN VIOLENCE IS PROBABLY AS BAD AS I'VE SEEN IT... IF IT IS NOT STOPPED, IT IS POSSIBLE THAT IRAQ COULD MOVE TOWARD CIVIL WAR.

121

AT THIS SAME TIME, VIOLENCE PERSISTED IN AFGHANISTAN. A SUICIDE CAR BOMBER IN A SMALL SOUTHERN TOWN KILLED HIMSELF AND 21 CIVILIANS, AND INJURED 14 OTHERS.

HOURS EARLIER IN A NEARBY AREA, 4 NATO SOLDIERS WERE KILLED AND 10 WOUNDED.

A TERRORIST PLOT TO BLOW UP AS MANY AS TEN COMMERCIAL AIRPLANES FLYING FROM BRITAIN TO THE U.S. AND CANADA WAS THWARTED BY BRITISH AUTHORITIES ON AUGUST 10. TWENTY-FOUR BRITISH-BORN MUSLIMS WERE ARRESTED, WHO PURPORTEDLY WERE TO CARRY OUT THE CONSPIRACY USING LIQUID-PEROXIDE-BASED EXPLOSIVES DISGUISED AS BEVERAGES.

AS BOMBINGS AND DEATHS CONTINUED IN IRAQ, NEW CASUALTY FIGURES RELEASED BY THE IRAQI HEALTH MINISTRY AND THE BAGHDAD MORGUE ON AUGUST 15 REVEALED THAT JULY HAD BEEN THE DEADLIEST MONTH OF THE WAR.

AN AVERAGE OF 110 IRAQIS WERE KILLED EACH DAY FOR A TOTAL OF 3,438 FOR THE MONTH.

AFTER 34 DAYS OF CONFLICT BETWEEN ISRAEL AND HEZBOLLAH, A UN-NEGOTIATED CEASE-FIRE WENT INTO EFFECT ON AUGUST 14.
FOUR HUNDRED CITIES AND VILLAGES WERE ATTACKED IN THE WAR, 50 IN ISRAEL AND 350 IN LEBANON.

ON AUGUST 17, IT WAS ANNOUNCED THAT ROADSIDE BOMBS IN IRAQ INCREASED IN JULY TO THE HIGHEST MONTHLY TOTAL SINCE THE START OF THE WAR.
IN JULY, 2,625 DEVICES WERE PLANTED AND 1,666 EXPLODED. IN CONTRAST, 1,454 WERE PLANTED IN JANUARY.

"THE INSURGENCY HAS GOTTEN WORSE," STATED AN UNNAMED SENIOR DEFENSE OFFICIAL.

FIRING FROM ROOFTOPS AND BUILDINGS, INSURGENTS KILLED 20 SHIITE PILGRIMS AND WOUNDED 300 PARADING THROUGH BAGHDAD FOR A RELIGIOUS FESTIVAL HELD ON AUGUST 20.

IN A *NEW YORK TIMES/CBS* POLL RELEASED ON AUGUST 23, THE FOLLOWING WERE FOUND...

51% SEE NO LINK BETWEEN IRAQ WAR AND BROAD ANTITERROR EFFORT

53% SAY GOING TO WAR IN IRAQ WAS A MISTAKE

62% SAY IRAQ WAR IS GOING BADLY

57% DISAPPROVE OF PRESIDENT'S ACTIONS
37% APPROVE
7% NO OPINION

IN A BLOODY CLASH BETWEEN THE IRAQI ARMY AND THE MILITIA OF RADICAL CLERIC MUQTADA AL-SADR ON AUGUST 28, 20 GUNMEN AND 8 CIVILIANS WERE KILLED AND 70 WERE WOUNDED.

THIS ENDED A VIOLENT TWO DAYS IN WHICH MORE THAN 100 IRAQIS WERE KILLED AS WELL AS 9 AMERICAN SERVICE PEOPLE.

NEVILLE CHAMBERLAIN

SPEAKING BEFORE THE AMERICAN LEGION IN SALT LAKE CITY ON AUGUST 29, DEFENSE SECRETARY RUMSFELD COMPARED CRITICS OF THE BUSH ADMINISTRATION TO NAZI APPEASERS PRIOR TO WORLD WAR II. HE STATED...

"ONCE AGAIN WE FACE SIMILAR CHALLENGES IN...A NEW TYPE OF FASCISM. BUT SOME SEEM NOT TO HAVE LEARNED HISTORY'S LESSONS."

AS VIOLENCE CONTINUED TO RESIST ATTEMPTS TO CURB IT, 65 MORE IRAQIS WERE SLAIN ON AUGUST 30. STILL, AMERICA'S TOP GENERAL IN IRAQ, GEORGE CASEY, STATED...

"OVER THE NEXT 12 TO 18 MONTHS, I CAN SEE THE IRAQI SECURITY FORCES PROGRESSING TO A POINT WHERE THEY CAN TAKE ON THE SECURITY RESPONSIBILITIES FOR THE COUNTRY WITH VERY LITTLE COALITION SUPPORT."

THE RISE OF SECTARIAN CLASHES AND THE GROWING STRENGTH OF THE SUNNI-BASED INSURGENCY IN IRAQ CAUSED A HUGE JUMP IN IRAQI CASUALTIES, ACCORDING TO A PENTAGON REPORT ISSUED ON SEPTEMBER 1. SINCE MAY 20 AND THE START OF THE NEW GOVERNMENT, AVERAGE WEEKLY ATTACKS ROSE FROM 423 IN EARLY 2004 TO 792 AT PRESENT. OTHER PENTAGON FIGURES FOLLOW:

120 AT PRESENT

80 MID-FEB. TO MID-MAY

30 TWO YEARS AGO

BODIES FOUND BY BAGHDAD CORONER'S OFFICE IN MONTH

1,600 JUNE

1,800 JULY

A STUDY BY NEW YORK'S MT. SINAI MEDICAL CENTER ISSUED IN EARLY SEPTEMBER DETERMINED THAT WORKERS AT GROUND ZERO ON 9/11 HAD BEEN MORE ADVERSELY AFFECTED THAN PREVIOUSLY BELIEVED. THE STUDY SAID THAT ABOUT 70% OF NEARLY 10,000 WORKERS TESTED REPORTED NEW OR WORSENED RESPIRATORY PROBLEMS. NEW YORK SENATOR HILLARY CLINTON COMMENTED...

"...THIS STUDY, I HOPE, PUTS TO REST ANY DOUBT ABOUT WHAT IS HAPPENING."

A REPORT BY THE SENATE INTELLIGENCE COMMITTEE ON SEPTEMBER 8 SAID THAT THE CIA HAD INFORMED THE ADMINISTRATION IN OCTOBER 2005 THAT SADDAM HUSSEIN HAD NO CONNECTION WITH AL QAEDA. YET THE ADMINISTRATION CONTINUED TO MAKE FALSE ACCUSATIONS. AS RECENTLY AS AUGUST 21, 2006, THE PRESIDENT SAID THAT HUSSEIN... "...HAD RELATIONS WITH ZARQAWI."

ON SEPTEMBER 10, VICE PRESIDENT CHENEY WAS ASKED IF HE HAD KNOWN THAT IRAQ DID NOT HAVE WEAPONS OF MASS DESTRUCTION, WOULD HE HAVE RECOMMENDED DIFFERENT ACTIONS. HE RESPONDED... "...WE'D DO EXACTLY THE SAME THING."

ON SEPTEMBER 18, ONE OF AFGHANISTAN'S DEADLIEST DAYS, THREE SUICIDE BOMBS EXPLODED, KILLING 18 PEOPLE AND WOUNDING MORE THAN 60. A FOURTH SUICIDE BOMBER CAUSED THE DEATH OF 4 CANADIAN SOLDIERS.

ON SEPTEMBER 20, A UN REPORT CLAIMED THAT 5,106 IRAQI CIVILIANS IN BAGHDAD DIED VIOLENT DEATHS DURING JULY AND AUGUST, FAR MORE THAN THE CITY'S MORGUE REPORTED.

BOTH PRESIDENT BUSH AND VICE PRESIDENT CHENEY CONTINUED TO STATE THAT THE WAR HAS MADE US SAFER.

A SWEEPING ASSESSMENT OF GLOBAL TERRORISM BY 16 U.S. INTELLIGENCE AGENCIES MADE PUBLIC ON SEPTEMBER 24 CLAIMED THAT THE AMERICAN WAR IN IRAQ HAD AIDED THE SPREAD OF ISLAMIC RADICALISM AND THAT THE THREAT OF TERRORISM HAD INCREASED SINCE 9/11.

ACCORDING TO BOB WOODWARD'S NEW BOOK, *STATE OF DENIAL*, PUBLISHED ON OCTOBER 2, PRESIDENT BUSH IGNORED WARNINGS BY ONE OF HIS FOREMOST ADVISERS IN SEPTEMBER 2003 THAT THOUSANDS OF MORE TROOPS WERE NEEDED IN IRAQ TO STOP THE INSURGENCY.

THE BOOK ALSO ASSERTED THAT CHIEF OF STAFF ANDREW CARD TWICE ATTEMPTED TO CONVINCE THE PRESIDENT TO FIRE DONALD RUMSFELD, ONCE WITH THE SUPPORT OF FIRST LADY LAURA BUSH.

JOHN ABIZAID IN FALL 2003 "RUMSFELD DOESN'T HAVE ANY CREDIBILITY ANYMORE."

COLIN POWELL, AFTER 2005 ELECTION "IF I GO, THEN DON SHOULD GO."

FORMER FIRST LADY BARBARA BUSH, IN JANUARY 2003... "[THE PRESIDENT'S FATHER] IS CERTAINLY WORRIED [ABOUT THE IRAQ INVASION] AND IS LOSING SLEEP OVER IT; HE'S UP AT NIGHT WORRIED..."

PRESIDENT BUSH IN NOVEMBER 2003... "I DON'T WANT ANYONE IN THE CABINET TO SAY IT IS AN INSURGENCY. I DON'T THINK WE ARE THERE YET."

AS SECTARIAN VIOLENCE AND KILLINGS OF COALITION FORCES CONTINUED IN IRAQ IN EARLY OCTOBER, PRIME MINISTER MALIKI ANNOUNCED A NEW SECURITY PLAN ON OCTOBER 9. THE PLAN WOULD UTILIZE COMMITTEES OF NEIGHBORHOOD LEADERS TO QUELL CRISES IN THEIR INDIVIDUAL AREAS.

THOUGH STILL VAGUE, THIS WAS AIMED PRIMARILY AT PROTECTING SUNNI IRAQIS AND U.S. AND BRITISH TROOPS. IN THE LAST THREE DAYS, 13 COALITION FORCES HAD BEEN KILLED.

ON OCTOBER 10, EIGHT GI'S WERE KILLED IN BAGHDAD, A SINGLE DAY'S BIGGEST TOTAL IN 15 MONTHS.

ON OCTOBER 10, A NEW STUDY BY U.S. AND IRAQI PUBLIC HEALTH RESEARCHERS ESTIMATED THAT 600,000 IRAQI CIVILIANS HAD DIED VIOLENT DEATHS SINCE THE INVASION IN 2003.

WHILE GRANTING THAT VIOLENCE IN BAGHDAD WAS AT ITS HIGHEST LEVEL IN WEEKS, GEN. GEORGE CASEY, AS WELL AS PRESIDENT BUSH, DISPUTED THE FIGURES, SAYING... "THE LEVELS OF VIOLENCE OVER THE LAST FEW WEEKS ARE AS HIGH AS THEY HAVE BEEN. BUT IT'S GOING TO GO BACK DOWN." (CASEY)
"I DON'T CONSIDER IT A CREDIBLE REPORT." (PRESIDENT BUSH)

ON OCTOBER 24, GENERAL CASEY SAID IT MIGHT BE NECESSARY TO INCREASE TROOP LEVELS IN BAGHDAD TO RECAPTURE THE STREETS. HE ALSO PREDICTED THAT IRAQI TROOPS COULD ASSUME THE MAIN WAR BURDEN IN 12 TO 18 MONTHS. AT THAT TIME, AMBASSADOR KHALILZAD SAID, SUCCESS IN IRAQ WAS POSSIBLE..."[BUT] IRAQI LEADERS MUST STEP UP TO ACHIEVE KEY POLITICAL AND SECURITY MILESTONES ON WHICH THEY HAVE AGREED."

AS OCTOBER CAME TO A CLOSE, THE AFGHANISTAN WAR HEATED UP. IN THREE DIFFERENT CLASHES, 163 TALIBAN INSURGENTS WERE KILLED BY NATO AND AFGHAN TROOPS.

IN IRAQ, AMERICAN MILITARY LOSSES FOR OCTOBER ROSE TO 102, THE HIGHEST MONTHLY TOTAL SINCE JANUARY 2005. VIOLENCE BY INSURGENTS ALSO CONTINUED AS 46 IRAQIS PERISHED IN SIX BOMBINGS.

U.S. SOLDIERS PLACED A CORDON AROUND SADR CITY TO HELP STEM THE VIOLENCE.

CONGRESSIONAL ELECTIONS ON NOVEMBER 7 GIVE THE DEMOCRATS CONTROL OF BOTH THE HOUSE AND SENATE (BY 51-49) FOR THE FIRST TIME SINCE 1994. CALIFORNIA REPRESENTATIVE NANCY PELOSI BECOMES THE FIRST WOMAN EVER ELECTED SPEAKER OF THE HOUSE, WHILE NEVADA SENATOR HARRY REID IS ELECTED SENATE MAJORITY LEADER.

ON NOVEMBER 5, THE IRAQI COURT JUDGING SADDAM HUSSEIN FOUND HIM GUILTY OF CRIMES AGAINST HUMANITY AND SENTENCED HIM TO DEATH BY HANGING.

FIFTY INSURGENT GUNMEN WEARING IRAQI POLICE COMMANDO UNIFORMS AND DRIVING VEHICLES WITH INTERIOR MINISTRY MARKINGS MARCHED INTO BAGHDAD'S MINISTRY OF HIGHER EDUCATION ON NOVEMBER 14 AND KIDNAPPED AT LEAST 55 WORKERS AND VISITORS.

HERDED INTO A FLEET OF TRUCKS, THEY WERE DRIVEN TOWARD MAINLY SHIITE NEIGHBORHOODS. PRIME MINISTER MALIKI DENIED THIS WAS TERRORISM, INSTEAD DESCRIBING IT AS "DISAGREEMENTS AND CONFLICTS BETWEEN MILITIAS BELONGING ON THIS SIDE OR THAT."

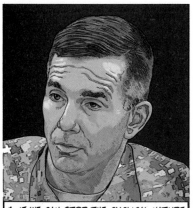

A REPORT RELEASED BY THE UN ON NOVEMBER 22 SAID THERE WERE 3,709 IRAQI CIVILIAN DEATHS IN OCTOBER, MORE THAN ANY PREVIOUS MONTH SINCE THE START OF THE WAR. MUCH OF THIS BLOODSHED WAS CAUSED BY ATTACKS AND COUNTER-ATTACKS BY SHIITES AND SUNNIS. TWO COMMENTS WERE...

"...IF WE CAN STOP THE CYCLICAL NATURE OF THIS IN BAGHDAD, WE COULD REALLY CHANGE THE DYNAMICS HERE..." SAID MAJ. GEN. WILLIAM B. CALDWELL IV, CHIEF SPOKESMAN FOR THE AMERICAN COMMAND IN IRAQ.

"WE HAVE A SITUATION IN WHICH IMPUNITY PREVAILS. IT'S CRITICALLY IMPORTANT FOR THE GOVERNMENT TO ENSURE THAT JUSTICE IS DONE..." SAID GIANNI MAGAZZENI, CHIEF OF THE UN'S HUMAN RIGHTS OFFICE IN BAGHDAD.

BUT DAYS LATER, BAGHDAD EXPERIENCED THE DEADLIEST SECTARIAN ATTACK SINCE THE WAR BEGAN. FIVE CAR BOMBS EXPLODED IN STREETS AND MARKETS OF THE SHIITE AREA OF SADR CITY, KILLING MORE THAN 144 AND WOUNDING OVER 200.

SHIITE REVENGE QUICKLY FOLLOWED, AS MORTARS WERE FIRED INTO SUNNI NEIGHBORHOODS AND ATTACKS WERE MADE ON FOUR SUNNI MOSQUES.

ON NOVEMBER 30, MEETING WITH PRIME MINISTER MALIKI IN JORDAN, PRESIDENT BUSH SAID THAT THE TROUBLE IN IRAQ WOULD NOT CAUSE THE U.S. TO WITHDRAW. MR. MALIKI, IN TURN, SAID HIS COUNTRY'S FORCES WOULD TAKE OVER RESPONSIBILITY IN JUNE.

"WE'RE GOING TO STAY IN IRAQ TO GET THE JOB DONE AS LONG AS THE GOVERNMENT WANTS US THERE..."

...DECLARED THE PRESIDENT.

"I CAN TELL YOU THAT BY NEXT JUNE OUR FORCES WILL BE READY..."

...SAID THE CONFIDENT PRIME MINISTER.

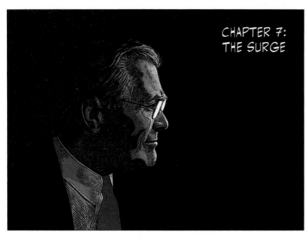

CHAPTER 7:
THE SURGE

REVERSING COURSE, PRESIDENT BUSH ACCEPTED DEFENSE SECRETARY RUMSFELD'S RESIGNATION ON DECEMBER 2. ROBERT GATES WAS NOMINATED TO REPLACE HIM.
RUMSFELD'S LAST MEMO WAS MADE PUBLIC. DATED NOVEMBER 6, IT READ IN PART...

"...IT IS TIME FOR A MAJOR ADJUSTMENT. CLEARLY, WHAT U.S. FORCES ARE CURRENTLY DOING IN IRAQ IS NOT WORKING WELL ENOUGH OR FAST ENOUGH... [IRAQIS] MUST PULL UP THEIR SOCKS, STEP UP AND TAKE RESPONSIBILITY FOR THEIR COUNTRY..."

A JOINT REPORT BY THE PENTAGON AND THE STATE DEPARTMENT, ISSUED ON DECEMBER 3, CRITICIZED AMERICAN FIELD TRAINING OF THE AFGHAN POLICE FORCE.

I CAN'T HANDLE THIS MANY, SIR. THEY'LL NEVER MAKE IT.

BLAMING AN INEFFECTUAL SLOW START AND UNDERSTAFFING, THE REPORT CALLED THE POLICE FORCE INCAPABLE OF CARRYING OUT ROUTINE LAW ENFORCEMENT.
THE BIPARTISAN IRAQ STUDY GROUP MADE 79 RECOMMENDATIONS TO THE PRESIDENT AND CONGRESS ON DECEMBER 6.
THEY LABELED THE SITUATION IN IRAQ "GRAVE AND DETERIORATING," SUGGESTED GREATER DIPLOMATIC EFFORTS WITH SYRIA AND IRAN, CALLED FOR A NEW APPROACH TO THE WAR, AND PROPOSED PULLING BACK ALL AMERICAN FORCES IN THE NEXT 15 MONTHS.

"THE CURRENT APPROACH IS NOT WORKING AND THE ABILITY OF THE U.S. TO INFLUENCE EVENTS IS DIMINISHING..."

...SAID CO-CHAIR LEE HAMILTON.

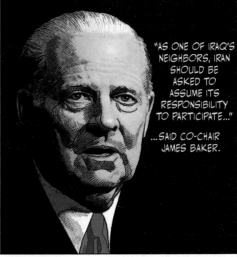

"AS ONE OF IRAQ'S NEIGHBORS, IRAN SHOULD BE ASKED TO ASSUME ITS RESPONSIBILITY TO PARTICIPATE..."

...SAID CO-CHAIR JAMES BAKER.

THE PRESIDENT QUICKLY RESPONDED, SAYING HE WOULD NOT PULL BACK TROOPS IN 15 MONTHS OR MEET WITH IRAN.

AS SECTARIAN VIOLENCE CONTINUED IN IRAQ, A TRUCK DROVE UP TO A CROWD OF SHIITE DAY LABORERS IN BAGHDAD ON DECEMBER 12, SUPPOSEDLY OFFERING WORK. INSTEAD IT EXPLODED, KILLING 70 AND WOUNDING 236 IN THE DISASTER.

SIXTY-ONE MORE WERE KILLED THAT DAY IN ALL OF IRAQ.

SPEAKING ON *FACE THE NATION* ON DECEMBER 17, FORMER SECRETARY OF STATE COLIN POWELL SAID HE DID NOT BELIEVE "THAT ANOTHER SURGE OF TROOPS INTO BAGHDAD" WOULD WORK AND THAT THE ARMY WAS "ABOUT BROKEN." HE ADDED…"IF I WERE STILL CHAIRMAN OF THE JOINT CHIEFS OF STAFF, MY FIRST QUESTION [WOULD BE]: WHAT MISSION IS IT THAT THESE TROOPS ARE TO ACCOMPLISH?"

POWELL ALSO ENDORSED MEETING WITH IRAN AND SYRIA.

VISITING IRAQ ON DECEMBER 21, HIS SECOND DAY IN OFFICE, NEW DEFENSE SECRETARY ROBERT M. GATES SAID THAT MILITARY COMMANDERS WERE CONCERNED THAT ADDED TROOPS COULD STALL THE IRAQI GOVERNMENT FROM TAKING RESPONSIBILITY FOR ITS OWN SECURITY.

A DAY LATER, FOUR U.S. MARINES WERE CHARGED WITH THE KILLING OF 24 IRAQI CIVILIANS IN THE VILLAGE OF HADITHA LAST YEAR. THE CRIMES ARE PUNISHABLE WITH LIFE IMPRISONMENT AND DISHONORABLE DISCHARGE.

FORMER PRESIDENT GERALD FORD DIES ON DECEMBER 26 AT THE AGE OF 93. THE 38TH PRESIDENT TOOK OVER FROM RICHARD NIXON IN 1974 WHEN THE PRESIDENT RESIGNED AFTER THE WATERGATE DISCLOSURES.

IN ONE OF THE MOST IMPORTANT ACTIONS BY BRITISH TROOPS, A COMBINED BRITISH-IRAQI FORCE STORMED A POLICE STATION IN BASRA IN LATE DECEMBER AND RESCUED 127 PRISONERS FROM TORTURE AND PROBABLE EXECUTION BY THE POLICE.

THIS WAS VIEWED AS AN EXAMPLE OF THE IRAQI POLICE BEING INFILTRATED BY CRIMINALS AND TERRORIZING MILITIAS LIKE MUQTADA AL-SADR'S MAHDI ARMY.

AFTER A LENGTHY AND STORMY TRIAL, SADDAM HUSSEIN WAS HANGED ON DECEMBER 29 IN BAGHDAD. THE FORMER IRAQI LEADER WAS 69 YEARS OLD.

"IT IS AN IMPORTANT MILESTONE ON IRAQ'S COURSE TO BECOMING A DEMOCRACY..."

...COMMENTED PRESIDENT BUSH.

ODIERNO

ON SUNDAY, DECEMBER 31, AMERICA'S FATALITIES IN THE IRAQ WAR REACHED THE GRIM TOTAL OF 3,000, WHEN 22-YEAR-OLD SPECIALIST DUSTIN R. DONICA, OF SPRING, TEXAS, WAS KILLED IN ACTION.

ACCORDING TO A RECENT PENTAGON REPORT, DECEMBER 2006 WAS THE THIRD-DEADLIEST MONTH FOR AMERICAN TROOPS SINCE THE WAR BEGAN, WITH 111 SOLDIERS KILLED. AMERICAN WOUNDED THUS FAR TOTALED MORE THAN 22,000.

LT. GEN. RAYMOND T. ODIERNO, AMERICA'S SECOND-RANKING COMMANDER IN IRAQ, SAID ON JANUARY 7 THAT EVEN WITH THE SURGE IN TROOPS, IT COULD TAKE "TWO OR THREE YEARS" MORE FOR U.S. AND IRAQI FORCES TO GAIN THE UPPER HAND IN THE WAR. HE WENT ON... "IF THEY [THE AMERICAN PEOPLE] FEEL WE ARE MAKING PROGRESS, THEY WILL HAVE THE PATIENCE."

I THINK THE FRUSTRATION IS THAT THEY THINK WE ARE NOT MAKING PROGRESS.

THE GENERAL CALLED FOR NEW TROOPS IN BAGHDAD TO WORK ALONGSIDE THREE IRAQI COMBAT BRIGADES, RETURN TO THE CITY'S TOUGHEST NEIGHBORHOODS, AND SHOW THEY CAN "PROTECT THE PEOPLE." SOMETHING, HE SAID, THEY HAD PREVIOUSLY FAILED TO DO.

MORE THAN 1,000 AMERICAN AND IRAQI FORCES SUPPORTED BY APACHE HELICOPTERS AND FIGHTER JETS FOUGHT INSURGENTS IN BAGHDAD ON JANUARY 9.

IN THE DAYLONG BATTLE, AT LEAST 50 INSURGENTS WERE KILLED BY THE COMBINED TROOPS.

BAGHDAD

IN A SPEECH ON JANUARY 10, PRESIDENT BUSH PROMISED 20,000 MORE AMERICAN TROOPS IN IRAQ IN AN EFFORT TO "CHANGE AMERICA'S COURSE" IN THE WAR. HE ADDED... "IF WE INCREASE OUR SUPPORT AT THIS CRUCIAL MOMENT AND HELP THE IRAQIS BREAK THE CURRENT CYCLE OF VIOLENCE... WE CAN HASTEN THE DAY OUR TROOPS BEGIN TO COME HOME."

DAYS LATER, AS NEW U.S. TROOPS BEGAN TO ARRIVE IN IRAQ, GEN. GEORGE CASEY WARNED THAT IT MIGHT TAKE MONTHS FOR REAL PROGRESS TO TAKE PLACE. HE SAID... "...THERE ARE NO GUARANTEES OF SUCCESS AND IT'S NOT GOING TO HAPPEN OVERNIGHT. I THINK YOU'LL SEE A GRADUAL EVOLUTION OVER THE NEXT TWO OR THREE MONTHS."

MEANWHILE, REPORTS CONTINUED OF PRIME MINISTER MALIKI'S OPPOSITION TO THE PLAN.

IN MID-JANUARY, THE UN RELEASED CASUALTY FIGURES OF IRAQI CIVILIAN DEATHS THAT WERE THREE TIMES HIGHER THAN THE IRAQI GOVERNMENT ESTIMATES. THE UN RECORDED 34,452 DEATHS IN 2006, NOT INCLUDING DECEMBER, OR AN AVERAGE OF 94 IRAQIS DEAD EACH DAY. THEY ALSO REPORTED THAT AT LEAST 470,094 IRAQIS HAD FLED THEIR HOMES SINCE LAST FEBRUARY.

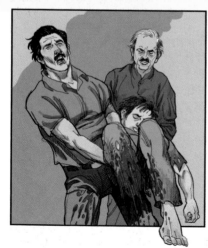

ON JANUARY 21, IN ONE OF THE WAR'S COSTLIEST DAYS FOR AMERICAN TROOPS, A U.S. HELICOPTER CRASHED IN BAGHDAD, KILLING ALL 13 SERVICE PEOPLE ABOARD.

THE TOTAL OF ALL MILITARY DEATHS IN IRAQ FOR THAT WEEKEND WAS 27.

AT LEAST 88 PEOPLE WERE KILLED AND 160 WOUNDED BY TWO CAR BOMBS EXPLODING IN A CROWDED BAGHDAD MARKET ON JANUARY 22, IN ONE OF THE WORST MASSACRES SINCE THE WAR'S BEGINNING.

LESS THAN TWO WEEKS LATER, AN ALMOST IDENTICAL BOMBING TOOK PLACE IN A MARKET IN HILLA, KILLING MORE THAN 60 AND WOUNDING 150.

ON JANUARY 30, OVER 250 MOSTLY SHIITE MILITANTS WERE KILLED BY AMERICAN AND IRAQI FORCES, BACKED BY U.S. HELICOPTERS AND TANKS, NEAR NAJAF IN A DEADLY BATTLE LASTING 15 HOURS.

ONE DAY LATER, IT WAS DISCLOSED THAT THE IRAQI FORCES WERE NEARLY OVERWHELMED AND NEEDED MORE AMERICAN AID THAN PREVIOUSLY REVEALED.

A REPORT TO CONGRESS BY THE 16 U.S. INTELLIGENCE AGENCIES ON FEBRUARY 2 SERIOUSLY DOUBTED THE COMPETENCE OF IRAQI POLITICIANS TO HOLD THE NATION TOGETHER.

THE ABILITY OF IRAQI TROOPS TO BE RESPONSIBLE FOR GREATER SECURITY IN THE NEXT 18 MONTHS WAS ALSO QUESTIONED BY THE REPORT.

CIVIL WAR IS CHECKERS... THIS IS CHESS.

ON FEBRUARY 3, THE CARNAGE GREW WORSE AS 135 WERE KILLED AND MORE THAN 300 WOUNDED BY A POWERFUL TRUCK BOMB EXPLODING AND DESTROYING A SHIITE MARKET IN BAGHDAD.

JOHN E. MCLAUGHLIN, FORMER ACTING DIRECTOR OF THE CIA

133

MAYHEM BY INSURGENTS CONTINUED IN IRAQ AS TWO BAGHDAD MARKETS WERE HIT BY FOUR BOMBS, KILLING AT LEAST 67 AND WOUNDING 155 ON FEBRUARY 12.

THE ATTACKS CAME ON THE ANNIVERSARY OF BOMBINGS THAT DESTROYED THE VENERATED GOLDEN MOSQUE IN SAMARRA, AN EVENT THAT HAS BEEN CALLED THE START OF THE SUNNI-SHIITE CIVIL WAR.

ON FEBRUARY 15, PRESIDENT BUSH WARNED THAT THE SNOW WOULD SOON BE MELTING IN THE AFGHAN MOUNTAINS AND "WE CAN EXPECT FIERCE FIGHTING TO CONTINUE."

ADMITTING THAT 2006 HAD BEEN A DIFFICULT YEAR FOR AFGHANISTAN AS WELL AS IRAQ, HE ASKED FOR GREATER NATO AID IN AFGHANISTAN. HE ALSO DECLARED,

"...WHEN THE COMMANDERS ON THE GROUND SAY TO OUR RESPECTIVE COUNTRIES...'WE NEED ADDITIONAL HELP'...OUR NATO COUNTRIES MUST PROVIDE IT IN ORDER TO BE SUCCESSFUL IN THIS MISSION."

"THE BUSH ADMINISTRATION TOOK ITS EYE OFF THE BALL IN AFGHANISTAN," STATED A DEMOCRATIC PARTY RESPONSE.

TWO CAR BOMBS WERE EXPLODED IN A BAGHDAD MARKET ON FEBRUARY 18, KILLING MORE THAN 60 PEOPLE. THIS OCCURRED TWO DAYS AFTER IRAQI PRIME MINISTER MALIKI TOLD PRESIDENT BUSH...

"THE SECURITY PLAN HAS BEEN A DAZZLING SUCCESS DURING ITS FIRST DAYS."

AFTER NEGOTIATING FOR MONTHS, A PLAN FOR INCREASING OIL PRODUCTION AND DISTRIBUTING REVENUE TO ALL GROUPS WAS SIGNED BY THE IRAQI GOVERNMENT ON FEBRUARY 26.

U.S. AMBASSADOR TO IRAQ ZALMAY KHALILZAD COMMENTED...
"...LEADERS REPRESENTING ALL OF IRAQ'S COMMUNITIES HAVE DEMONSTRATED THAT THEY CAN PULL TOGETHER TO RESOLVE DIFFICULT ISSUES."

IN AN APPARENT POLICY SHIFT, THE U.S. AGREED ON FEBRUARY 27 TO JOIN HIGH-LEVEL TALKS ON IRAQ WITH IRAN AND SYRIA, ALONG WITH BRITAIN, RUSSIA, AND OTHER MIDDLE EASTERN NATIONS.
SECRETARY OF STATE RICE DECLARED...

"...THIS IS ONE OF THE KEY FINDINGS, OF COURSE, OF THE IRAQ STUDY GROUP. WE'VE LEARNED, AND I WANT YOU TO KNOW THAT."

ON MARCH 5, A SUICIDE CAR BOMBER EXPLODED IN THE POPULAR MUTANABI STREET BOOK MARKET IN BAGHDAD, KILLING 30 AND WOUNDING MORE THAN 65.
A DAY LATER, 117 SHIITES WERE KILLED AND 170 WOUNDED IN VARIOUS ATTACKS, THE SEVENTH DAY OF MAJOR BOMBINGS SINCE THE START OF THE SECURITY DRIVE THREE DAYS EARLIER.

LEWIS LIBBY, FORMER CHIEF OF STAFF TO VICE PRESIDENT CHENEY, IS FOUND GUILTY ON FOUR COUNTS OF PERJURY AND OBSTRUCTION OF JUSTICE IN THE CASE INVOLVING THE IDENTITY LEAK OF CIA AGENT VALERIE PLAME WILSON.

ACCORDING TO A MARCH 14 PENTAGON REPORT, THE UTILIZATION OF IRAQI MILITARY FORCES HAD DECLINED APPRECIABLY SINCE OCTOBER. IN THAT MONTH, U.S. FORCES CONDUCTED 8% OF COMBAT OPERATIONS WHILE 72% WERE CONDUCTED BY JOINT FORCES.
IN JANUARY, U.S. TROOPS CONDUCTED 33% OF OPERATIONS WHILE JOINT OPERATIONS FELL TO 59%.

MARKING THE FOURTH ANNIVERSARY OF THE INVASION OF IRAQ ON MARCH 19 WHILE STANDING IN FRONT OF RIBBONS COMMEMORATING FAMOUS AMERICAN BATTLES, PRESIDENT BUSH ONCE AGAIN DECLARED THE WAR "CAN BE WON."
HE ADDED...

IF AMERICAN FORCES WERE TO STEP BACK FROM BAGHDAD... THE VIOLENCE WOULD ENGULF THE REGION.

"AFTER FOUR YEARS OF FAILURE IN IRAQ," COUNTERED SENATE MAJORITY LEADER HARRY REID, "THE PRESIDENT'S ONLY ANSWER IS TO DO MORE OF THE SAME."

AN ARTICLE IN *THE NEW YORK TIMES* ON MARCH 26 CONTRASTED THE EXTREME DIFFERENCES BETWEEN SUNNI AND SHIITE NEIGHBORHOODS IN IRAQ AND DECLARED THAT THE PRESENT CIVIL WAR PITTED SUNNI AGAINST SUNNI AS WELL AS AGAINST SHIITE.

SUNNI AREAS ARE FILLED WITH DESTROYED BUILDINGS AND MOSQUES, STREETS MARRED BY MORTAR SHELLS, UNCOLLECTED TRASH, AND LITTLE ELECTRICITY. SHIITE AREAS HAVE MARKETS IN FULL SWING, CIVIL PROJECTS UNDER WAY, AND RELATIVE PEACE.

A TRUCK BOMBING IN TAL AFAR ON MARCH 27 KILLED 152 CIVILIANS AND WOUNDED 347, MOST OF THEM SHIITES. THIS WAS THE HIGHEST NUMBER OF CASUALTIES FROM A SINGLE BOMB IN THE WAR. IMMEDIATE REPRISALS BY SHIITES LEFT ANOTHER 47 DEAD.

BLAM-M!

ON APRIL 9, THE FOURTH ANNIVERSARY OF THE FALL OF BAGHDAD, TENS OF THOUSANDS OF PROTESTERS LOYAL TO MUQTADA AL-SADR MARCHED IN NAJAF CHANTING, "DEATH TO AMERICA," AND BURNING AMERICAN FLAGS.

ON APRIL 16, A MASSACRE ON THE VIRGINIA TECH CAMPUS COMMITTED BY 23-YEAR-OLD CHO SEUNG-HUI, A TROUBLED STUDENT, KILLED 32 STUDENTS AND WOUNDED 26. THE GUNMAN THEN KILLED HIMSELF IN THIS DEADLIEST CAMPUS INCIDENT IN U.S. HISTORY.

APRIL 18 BECAME THE DEADLIEST DAY SINCE THE START OF THE AMERICAN-LED SECURITY PLAN WHEN FIVE HORRIFIC BOMBINGS IN BAGHDAD, AIMED MAINLY AT SHIITE CROWDS, KILLED MORE THAN 172 AND INJURED OVER 200.

ON APRIL 19, AS CONGRESSIONAL DEMOCRATS SOUGHT TO PREPARE AN IRAQ WAR-SPENDING BILL, SENATE MAJORITY LEADER HARRY REID SAID...

THE WAR IS LOST.

THE SURGE IS NOT ACCOMPLISHING ANYTHING, AS INDICATED BY THE EXTREME VIOLENCE IN IRAQ.

ONE DAY LATER, DEFENSE SECRETARY ROBERT GATES ASKED THE IRAQI PARLIAMENT TO PASS LEGISLATION TO EASE SECTARIAN TENSIONS BEFORE THEY TOOK THEIR TWO-MONTH SUMMER HOLIDAY. GATES ADDED...

OUR COMMITMENT TO IRAQ IS LONG TERM... BUT IT IS NOT A COMMITMENT TO HAVE OUR YOUNG MEN AND WOMEN PATROLLING IRAQI STREETS OPEN-ENDEDLY.

ON APRIL 22, VIOLENCE IN IRAQ OPENED A NEW CHAPTER AS 21 MEMBERS OF A NON-MUSLIM MINORITY, AN ANCIENT SECT KNOWN AS YAZIDIS, WERE DRAGGED OFF A BUS IN MOSUL AND SHOT TO DEATH.

AT THE CENTER OF THE STORM, BY FORMER CIA DIRECTOR GEORGE TENET, PUBLISHED IN LATE APRIL, ACCUSED PRESIDENT BUSH AND VICE PRESIDENT CHENEY OF PRESSING THE NATION INTO THE IRAQ WAR WITHOUT A "SERIOUS DEBATE" ON ITS NECESSITY.
THE BOOK SAID THAT THE ADMINISTRATION'S CLAIM OF AN AL QAEDA-IRAQ LINK WAS "WAY BEYOND WHAT THE INTELLIGENCE SHOWS." AS TO WHETHER AN INCREASE IN TROOPS WOULD BE SUCCESSFUL, HE WROTE...

"...IT MAY HAVE WORKED THREE YEARS AGO. MY FEAR IS THAT SECTARIAN VIOLENCE HAS TAKEN ON A LIFE OF ITS OWN AND THAT U.S. FORCES ARE BECOMING MORE AND MORE IRRELEVANT TO THE MANAGEMENT OF THAT VIOLENCE."

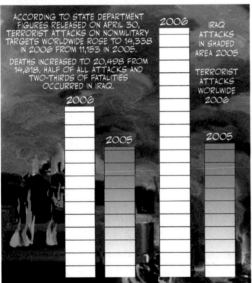

ACCORDING TO STATE DEPARTMENT FIGURES RELEASED ON APRIL 30, TERRORIST ATTACKS ON NONMILITARY TARGETS WORLDWIDE ROSE TO 14,338 IN 2006 FROM 11,153 IN 2005.

DEATHS INCREASED TO 20,498 FROM 14,618. HALF OF ALL ATTACKS AND TWO-THIRDS OF FATALITIES OCCURRED IN IRAQ.

2006

IRAQ ATTACKS IN SHADED AREA 2005

TERRORIST ATTACKS WORLWIDE 2006

2006

2005

2005

ON MAY 8, SIX MUSLIM MEN FROM NEW JERSEY AND PENNSYLVANIA, THREE OF WHOM WERE BROTHERS, WERE ARRESTED AND CHARGED WITH PLOTTING TO ATTACK FORT DIX IN NEW JERSEY WITH AUTOMATIC WEAPONS. THE FBI HAD BEEN TRACKING THEM FOR 15 MONTHS.

FORMER PRESIDENT JIMMY CARTER ON MAY 19 TOLD THE ARKANSAS DEMOCRAT-GAZETTE...
"... THE ALMOST UNDEVIATING SUPPORT BY GREAT BRITAIN FOR THE ILL-ADVISED POLICIES OF PRESIDENT BUSH IN IRAQ HAS BEEN A MAJOR TRAGEDY FOR THE WORLD."
CARTER ADDED, THE BUSH PRESIDENCY IS "THE WORST IN HISTORY."

THE SENATE INTELLIGENCE COMMITTEE ON MAY 25 CLAIMED THAT TWO MONTHS PRIOR TO THE INVASION OF IRAQ, INTELLIGENCE AGENCIES WARNED ON TWO DIFFERENT OCCASIONS THAT ESTABLISHING A DEMOCRACY IN IRAQ WOULD BE DIFFICULT AND WOULD HELP AL QAEDA INCREASE ITS OPERATION.
CHAIRMAN JOHN D. ROCKEFELLER SAID..."SADLY, THE ADMINISTRATION'S REFUSAL TO HEED THESE WARNINGS...HAS LED TO TRAGIC CONSEQUENCES FOR WHICH OUR NATION IS PAYING A TERRIBLE PRICE."

ON MAY 31, IN THE CONTINUING WAR IN AFGHANISTAN, 16 AFGHAN POLICEMEN WERE KILLED AND 6 WOUNDED IN AN AMBUSH WHILE DRIVING TOWARD KABUL. THE POLICE FOUGHT BACK, KILLING 10 MILITANTS AND WOUNDING OTHERS.

HEAVY FIGHTING HAS OCCURRED WITH RESURGENT TALIBAN FIGHTERS IN SEVERAL AREAS OF THE NATION.

IN EARLY JUNE, THREE MONTHS SINCE THE START OF THE BAGHDAD SECURITY PLAN INCREASING AMERICAN AND IRAQI TROOP PRESENCE IN THE CITY BY THE THOUSANDS, THE MILITARY CONTROLLED LESS THAN ONE-THIRD OF THE CITY'S NEIGHBORHOODS.
IT HAD BEEN EXPECTED THAT BAGHDAD NEIGHBORHOODS WOULD BE UNDER CONTROL IN JULY.
NOW THE GOAL WAS SEPTEMBER.

ON JUNE 5, A SUICIDE BOMBER'S TRUCK EXPLODED ON A COMMERCIAL STREET KILLING 18 AND WOUNDING AT LEAST 15. THROUGHOUT BAGHDAD, 33 BODIES WERE FOUND. MOST SHOT IN THE HEAD.

ON JUNE 10, TWO AMERICAN GENERALS--LT. GEN. MARTIN DEMPSEY AND MAJ. GEN. RICK LYNCH-- GAVE POOR GRADES TO IRAQI SECURITY FORCES FOR THEIR LACK OF READINESS.

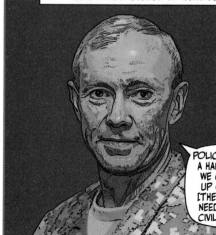

BOTH CLAIMED THAT THE NATIONAL POLICE FORCE WAS RIDDLED WITH CORRUPTION AND SECTARIANISM.

POLICE HAVE BEEN A HANDFUL, BUT WE CAN'T GIVE UP ON THEM... [THE COUNTRY] NEEDS TO HAVE CIVIL SECURITY.

LEWIS LIBBY IS SENTENCED ON JUNE 5 TO 30 MONTHS IN PRISON AND A FINE OF $250,000 FOR LYING IN THE VALERIE PLAME WILSON CASE. HOWEVER, ON JULY 2, PRESIDENT BUSH COMMUTES HIS SENTENCE BUT MAINTAINS THE FINE.
THE FORMER AIDE TO THE VICE PRESIDENT IS TO BE ON PROBATION FOR TWO YEARS.

ADM. WILLIAM J. FALLON, TOP AMERICAN COMMANDER IN THE MIDDLE EAST, SUGGESTED TO IRAQI PRIME MINISTER MALIKI ON JUNE 11 THAT POLITICAL PROGRESS NEEDED TO BE MADE BY NEXT MONTH TO COUNTER GROWING AMERICAN OPPOSITION TO THE WAR. HE SAID A LAW DIVIDING OIL PROFITS WOULD BE A PLACE TO START. FALLON TOLD HIM...
"YOU HAVE THE POWER...YOU SHOULD TAKE THE INITIATIVE."

DAYS LATER, DEFENSE SECRETARY GATES ALSO CRITICIZED THE SLOW PACE OF RECONCILIATION IN IRAQ UNDER MALIKI. HIS MESSAGE TO THE IRAQI GOVERNMENT WAS... "OUR TROOPS ARE BORROWING THEM TIME TO PURSUE RECONCILIATION...AND FRANKLY WE ARE DISAPPOINTED IN THE PROGRESS THUS FAR."

THIS LACK OF CONCILIATION WAS GRIMLY ACTED OUT IN IRAQ WHEN TWO EXPLOSIONS BY SUNNI EXTREMISTS DESTROYED THE TWIN MINARETS OF THE ALREADY DAMAGED SHIITE ASKARIYA MOSQUE IN SAMARRA ON JUNE 13, 2007.
THIS WAS FOLLOWED, ON JUNE 15, BY THE DESTRUCTION OF A LARGE SUNNI MOSQUE NEAR BASRA.
AND SEVERAL DAYS LATER, A PART OF THE SHIITE KHALANI MOSQUE IN BAGHDAD WAS DESTROYED BY A SUICIDE BOMBER KILLING MORE THAN 61 PEOPLE AND WOUNDING AT LEAST 130.

AS EXPECTED, PRIME MINISTER TONY BLAIR HANDED OVER THE LEADERSHIP OF THE LABOUR PARTY AND THE REINS OF GOVERNMENT TO FINANCE MINISTER GORDON BROWN ON JUNE 27.
BROWN, WHO PLEDGED THAT BRITAIN WOULD "MEET OUR INTERNATIONAL OBLIGATIONS," CALLED FOR GOING BEYOND MILITARY SOLUTIONS IN FIGHTING TERRORISM.
"IT IS ALSO," HE ADDED, "A STRUGGLE OF IDEAS AND IDEALS THAT IN THE COMING YEARS... WILL BE WAGED AND WON FOR HEARTS AND MINDS AT HOME AND ROUND THE WORLD."

AT LEAST 150 CIVILIANS WERE KILLED BY A SUICIDE TRUCK BOMB EXPLODING IN AN IMPOVERISHED SHIITE VILLAGE NORTH OF BAGHDAD ON JULY 8.

THIS SUGGESTED THAT INSURGENTS FLEEING THE U.S. MILITARY BUILDUP IN THE CAPITAL WERE TURNING TO TARGETS ELSEWHERE.

ON JULY 9, IRAQI FOREIGN MINISTER HOSHYAR ZEBARI SAID HIS COUNTRY WOULD SPLINTER INTO WARRING SEGMENTS IF AMERICAN TROOPS LEFT BEFORE IRAQI SECURITY FORCES WERE READY. HE ADDED...

THERE IS RISING SPECULATION ABOUT THE STABILITY OF THE GOVERNMENT. THESE SPECULATIONS ARE EXAGGERATED.

THIS WAS A DAY WHEN MORE THAN 50 CIVILIANS WERE KILLED IN SECTARIAN VIOLENCE.

IN MID-JULY, AMID MIXED REPORTS ON THE VALUE OF THE TROOP SURGE IN IRAQ, PRESIDENT BUSH ASKED CONGRESS TO WAIT UNTIL SEPTEMBER TO JUDGE THE STRATEGY. SO FAR, AMERICAN CASUALTIES IN 2007 WERE...

JANUARY-- 81
FEBRUARY-- 80
MARCH-- 80
APRIL-- 102
MAY-- 126
JUNE-- 101

IRAQI PRIME MINISTER MALIKI BOLDLY PRAISED THE CAPABILITIES OF HIS NATION'S MILITARY FORCES ON JULY 14. HE SAID... "WE ARE ABLE, GOD WILLING, TO TAKE THE RESPONSIBILITY COMPLETELY IN RUNNING THE SECURITY FILE IF THE INTERNATIONAL FORCES WITHDRAW."

TWO DAYS LATER, BOMBINGS KILLED MORE THAN 76 CIVILIANS IN THE OIL-RICH CITY OF KIRKUK.

A NEW REPORT BY THE 16 U.S. INTELLIGENCE AGENCIES ON JULY 17 DECLARED THAT AL QAEDA HAD "REGENERATED KEY ELEMENTS" OF ITS ABILITY TO ATTACK TARGETS IN THE U.S.
IT ALSO SAID THAT AL QAEDA "WILL PROBABLY SEEK TO LEVERAGE" THE CAPABILITIES OF THE IRAQI-BASED GROUP AL QAEDA IN IRAQ.

PRESIDENT BUSH INTERPRETED THE REPORT AS EVIDENCE THAT AL QAEDA WAS "...NOT NEARLY AS STRONG AS THEY WERE [BEFORE SEPTEMBER 11]," WHILE CALIFORNIA DEMOCRATIC REPRESENTATIVE JANE HARMAN SAID...

...THE THREAT HERE IS INCREASING AND PART OF IT RELATES TO THE STRENGTH OF AL QAEDA IN IRAQ.

A THREAT THAT POSTDATES OUR MILITARY ACTION IN IRAQ.

ON JULY 19, THE BUSH ADMINISTRATION AND MILITARY OFFICERS SAID THAT THOUGH THE SEPTEMBER REPORT WOULD SHOW PROGRESS IN IRAQ, THE SURGE COULD NOT BE ASSESSED UNTIL NOVEMBER.
LT. GEN. RAYMOND ODIERNO, NUMBER TWO COMMANDER IN IRAQ, DECLARED...

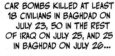

...IF I HAVE 45 MORE DAYS OF LOOKING AT THOSE TRENDS, I'LL BE ABLE TO MAKE A BIT MORE ACCURATE ASSESSMENT.

CAR BOMBS KILLED AT LEAST 18 CIVILIANS IN BAGHDAD ON JULY 23, 50 IN THE REST OF IRAQ ON JULY 25, AND 25 IN BAGHDAD ON JULY 26...

...THOUGH U.S. MILITARY DEATHS IN JULY WERE 74, THE LOWEST TOTAL IN 2007.

THE IRAQI PARLIAMENT HELD ITS FINAL SESSION ON JULY 30 BEFORE IT TOOK A MONTHLONG RECESS FOR THE SUMMER.
THEY HAD YET TO PASS LAWS CONCERNING THE SHARING OF OIL REVENUES, THE REINTEGRATION OF BAATHISTS, OR PROVINCIAL ELECTIONS.
THESE WERE ALL LEGISLATIONS THE U.S. CONGRESS HAD DESIGNATED AS BENCHMARKS.

ON AUGUST 2, DEFENSE SECRETARY GATES ADMITTED DISCOURAGEMENT BY THE AUGUST 1 RESIGNATION OF SUNNIS FROM THE IRAQI CABINET AND SAID THE ADMINISTRATION MIGHT HAVE UNDERESTIMATED THE DIFFICULTIES IN ACHIEVING SECTARIAN RECONCILIATION. HE ADDED...

"THE KEY IS NOT ONLY ESTABLISHING THE SECURITY BUT BEING ABLE TO HOLD ON TO THOSE AREAS...AND FOR THE IRAQI ARMY AND POLICE TO BE ABLE TO PROVIDE THE CONTINUITY OF SECURITY OVER TIME."

GIANTS SLUGGER BARRY BONDS HITS HIS 756TH HOME RUN ON AUGUST 7, BREAKING HANK AARON'S LIFETIME RECORD OF HOMERS. BONDS RECEIVES MIXED REACTIONS BECAUSE OF HIS ALLEGED USE OF STEROIDS.

IN THE DEADLIEST ATTACK OF THE IRAQ WAR, FOUR TRUCK BOMBS KILLED MORE THAN 400 AND WOUNDED 1,500 IN TWO KURDISH VILLAGES NEAR THE SYRIAN BORDER ON AUGUST 14. THE VICTIMS WERE MEMBERS OF THE YAZIDI SECT, A MINORITY GROUP OFTEN TARGETED BY SUNNIS.

EXPLOSIONS CAME ONLY HOURS AFTER IRAQI LEADERS MET UNSUCCESSFULLY TO SOLVE SECTARIAN DIFFERENCES.

A DAMNING REPORT BY THE CIA INSPECTOR GENERAL, KEPT SECRET FOR TWO YEARS, WAS MADE PUBLIC IN MID-AUGUST. IT CLAIMED THE AGENCY NEVER DEVELOPED A PLAN TO CONFRONT AL QAEDA BEFORE 9/11, THAT 2 OF THE 11 HIJACKERS WERE KNOWN TO BE IN THE U.S. BY MORE THAN 50 OFFICIALS AND NEVER ACTED ON, AND THAT THE UNIT TRACKING BIN LADIN "DID NOT HAVE THE TRAINING TO DO SO." FORMER CIA DIRECTOR GEORGE TENET COUNTERED...

...FOR ME, THERE WAS NO PRIORITY HIGHER THAN FIGHTING TERRORISM. [THE REPORT] VASTLY UNDERESTIMATES THE CHALLENGES FACED AND HEROIC PERFORMANCES OF THE HARDWORKING MEN AND WOMEN OF THE CIA.

COMPARING THE WAR IN IRAQ TO THE ONE IN VIETNAM, PRESIDENT BUSH TOLD THE VFW ON AUGUST 22...

...THEN AS NOW PEOPLE ARGUED THAT THE REAL PROBLEM WAS AMERICA'S PRESENCE... THE WORLD WOULD LEARN JUST HOW COSTLY THOSE MISREPRESENTATIONS WOULD BE.

HE ADDED, "PRIME MINISTER MALIKI IS A GOOD GUY... AND I SUPPORT HIM."

ONE DAY LATER, AN APPRAISAL BY THE 16 U.S. INTELLIGENCE AGENCIES CALLED THE IRAQI GOVERNMENT INCAPABLE OF GAINING FROM THE SURGE AND QUESTIONED THE PRESIDENT'S STRATEGY AS WELL AS THAT OF THE DEMOCRATS. SENATOR HILLARY CLINTON COMMENTED... "WE NEED TO STOP REFEREEING THIS CIVIL WAR AND START GETTING OUT NOW."

ACCORDING TO DATA FROM TWO HUMANITARIAN GROUPS PRESENTED IN LATE AUGUST, THE NUMBER OF IRAQIS FLEEING THEIR HOMES HAD SOARED SINCE THE SURGE BEGAN IN FEBRUARY.
MARCH 2006-- .005 MILLION
AUGUST 2006-- .02 MILLION
JANUARY 2007-- .045 MILLION
FEBRUARY 2007-- .05 MILLION
JULY 2007-- 1.1 MILLION

ON AUGUST 26, IRAQI PRIME MINISTER MALIKI LASHED OUT AT U.S. POLITICIANS CALLING FOR HIS RESIGNATION AND ACCUSED U.S. FORCES OF KILLING INNOCENT CITIZENS IN THEIR HUNT FOR INSURGENTS. HE ALSO PREDICTED THAT THE SEPTEMBER REPORT CARD WOULD BE... "...SUPPORTIVE OF THE GOVERNMENT."

ON AUGUST 27, AFTER MONTHS OF CRITICISM FROM THE HOUSE AND SENATE STEMMING FROM THE APPARENT POLITICIZING OF THE JUSTICE DEPT., ATTORNEY GENERAL ALBERTO GONZALES ANNOUNCES HIS RESIGNATION.

VIOLENCE CONTINUED IN IRAQ THROUGH AUGUST, AS A SUICIDE BOMBER DETONATED EXPLOSIVES HIDDEN IN HIS VEST INSIDE A SUNNI MOSQUE. TEN WERE KILLED AND MANY WERE WOUNDED.

AND THOUGH AGREEMENT WAS REACHED IN PARLIAMENT TO RETURN FORMER BAATHISTS TO GOVERNMENT JOBS AND SUNNI LEADER TAREQ AL-HASHEMI SAID HE WAS IMPRESSED, HIS GROUP WAS STILL UNWILLING TO RETURN TO THE LEGISLATURE.

A QUICK YEARLY REPORT ON THE CHANGING STATISTICS IN IRAQ, AS REPORTED BY *THE NEW YORK TIMES*:

	8/03	8/04	8/05	8/06	8/07
U.S. TROOPS IN IRAQ					
	139,000	140,000	138,000	138,000	162,000
FOREIGN TROOPS IN IRAQ					
	22,000	24,000	23,000	19,000	12,000
IRAQI SECURITY FORCES					
	35,000	91,000	183,000	298,000	360,000
DAILY ATTACKS BY INSURGENTS AND MILITIAS					
	18	77	70	160	120
IRAQI CIVILIANS DISPLACED BY VIOLENCE					
	25,000	25,000	15,000	100,000	80,000
OIL PRODUCTION IN MILLIONS OF BARRELS PER DAY PREWAR: UP TO 2.5					
	1.4	2.1	2.2	2.2	1.7
ELECTRICITY PRODUCTION (AVERAGE GIGAWATTS, PREWAR: 4.0)					
	3.3	4.7	4.0	4.4	4.1
IRAQIS SUPPORTING STRONG CENTRAL GOVERNMENT					
	85%	80%	70%	65%	55%

AFTER MEETING WITH MILITARY AND CIVILIAN OFFICIALS IN IRAQ ON SEPTEMBER 3, PRESIDENT BUSH DECLARED...

IF THE KIND OF SUCCESS WE ARE SEEING HERE CONTINUES, IT WILL BE POSSIBLE TO MAINTAIN THE SAME LEVEL OF SECURITY WITH FEWER AMERICAN FORCES. THESE DECISIONS WILL BE BASED ON A CALM ASSESSMENT BY OUR OWN MILITARY COMMANDERS.

ON SEPTEMBER 4, DAVID W. WALKER, HEAD OF THE U.S. ACCOUNTABILITY OFFICE, TOLD THE SENATE FOREIGN RELATIONS COMMITTEE THAT HE QUESTIONED WHETHER IRAQI POLICE AND MILITARY COULD MAINTAIN THE IMPROVEMENTS MADE BY THE SURGE. HE CALLED IT...

...AN IMPROVEMENT, BUT IT'S SEPARATE AND DISTINCT AS TO WHETHER IT'S SUSTAINABLE.

AS HEARINGS CONTINUED IN THE CAPITOL, ON SEPTEMBER 6, AN INDEPENDENT COMMISSION OF MILITARY EXPERTS LED BY RETIRED MARINE GENERAL JAMES L. JONES HAD AN ANSWER FOR EACH SIDE OF THE SENATE AISLE...

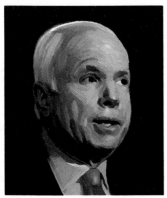

...I THINK DEADLINES CAN WORK AGAINST US.

...IF WE TAKE AWAY DEADLINES, WE TAKE AWAY BENCHMARKS, WHAT IS THE URGENCY THAT WILL MOVE THEM TO ACT?

ON SEPTEMBER 10, IN HIS LONG-ANTICIPATED APPEARANCE BEFORE CONGRESS TO DELIVER HIS OBJECTIVE APPRAISAL OF THE AMERICAN POSITION IN IRAQ AFTER THE JANUARY SURGE OF TROOPS, GEN. DAVID H. PETRAEUS, SENIOR AMERICAN COMMANDER IN IRAQ, WARNED AGAINST A RAPID PULLBACK. FACING LONG AND COMBATIVE QUESTIONING, HE STATED... "THE SITUATION IN IRAQ REMAINS COMPLEX, DIFFICULT, AND SOMETIMES DOWNRIGHT FRIGHTENING. I ALSO BELIEVE WE CAN ACHIEVE OUR OBJECTIVES IN IRAQ OVER TIME. ALTHOUGH DOING SO WILL BE NEITHER QUICK NOR EASY."

HE ALSO SAID HE HAD RECOMMENDED A WITHDRAWAL OF 30,000 TROOPS BY NEXT JULY.

DEMOCRATS IMMEDIATELY TOOK ISSUE...

SENATE MAJORITY LEADER HARRY REID SAID...

U.S. NATIONAL SECURITY REQUIRES THAT WE TRULY AND IMMEDIATELY CHANGE COURSE IN IRAQ.

AND SPEAKER OF THE HOUSE NANCY PELOSI SAID THE PRESIDENT...

...MUST EXPLAIN WHY OUR COUNTRY MUST CONTINUE TO MAKE THAT COMMITMENT.

A BENCHMARK SET BY THE ADMINISTRATION FOR JUDGING THE IRAQI GOVERNMENT'S CAPABILITIES SEEMED TO BE FALLING APART ON SEPTEMBER 12. KURDS AND SHIITES WHO HAD APPARENTLY AGREED ON AN OIL-SHARING MEASURE WERE NOW SHARPLY AT ODDS. IRAQI OIL MINISTER HUSSEIN AL- SHAHRISTANI SAID...

...THIS TO US INDICATES VERY SERIOUS LACK OF COOPERATION THAT MAKES MANY PEOPLE WONDER....IF THEY ARE REALLY GOING TO BE WORKING WITHIN THE FRAMEWORK OF THE FEDERAL LAW.

ON SEPTEMBER 13, PRESIDENT BUSH SUGGESTED AN "ENDURING RELATIONSHIP" WITH IRAQ AND KEEPING OUR FORCES THERE "BEYOND MY PRESIDENCY." HE ADDED...

THE MORE SUCCESSFUL WE ARE, THE MORE AMERICAN TROOPS CAN COME HOME.

A SHORT HISTORY OF THE IRAQ WAR

MARCH 20, 2003: THREE DAYS AFTER PRESIDENT BUSH GIVES SADDAM HUSSEIN 48 HOURS TO GIVE UP HIS POWER, THE U.S. BEGINS THE INVASION OF IRAQ.

MAY 1, 2003: BUSH DECLARES, "MAJOR COMBAT OPERATIONS IN IRAQ HAVE ENDED," WHILE STANDING UNDER A BANNER READING "MISSION ACCOMPLISHED."

DECEMBER 13, 2003: SADDAM HUSSEIN IS CAPTURED HIDING IN A HOLE IN THE GROUND NEAR TIKRIT. HE IS HANGED THREE YEARS LATER AFTER A LENGTHY TRIAL.

APRIL 2004: PHOTOGRAPHS OF PRISONER ABUSE AT U.S-RUN ABU GHRAIB PRISON OUTSIDE BAGHDAD ARE FOUND.

JUNE 28, 2004: GOVERNMENTAL POWER IN IRAQ IS TURNED OVER TO AN IRAQI INTERIM GOVERNMENT.

OCTOBER 6, 2004: TOP U.S. ARMS INSPECTOR IN IRAQ FINDS NO EVIDENCE THAT HUSSEIN'S GOVERNMENT PRODUCED WEAPONS OF MASS DESTRUCTION.

MAY 3, 2005: FIRST DEMOCRATICALLY ELECTED GOVERNMENT IN IRAQ IS SWORN IN.

FEBRUARY 22, 2006: BOMBERS DESTROY THE DOME OF A REVERED SHIITE MOSQUE IN SAMARRA, WHICH MANY CONSIDER THE START OF A FULL IRAQI CIVIL WAR. THE NEXT DAY, MORE THAN 136 IRAQIS ARE KILLED IN SECTARIAN VIOLENCE.

NOVEMBER 7, 2006: REPUBLICANS LOSE CONTROL OF BOTH HOUSES OF CONGRESS IN WHAT IS VIEWED AS A REFERENDUM ON THE WAR.

NOVEMBER 8, 2006: DEFENSE SECRETARY DONALD RUMSFELD RESIGNS HIS OFFICE AND ROBERT GATES IS NAMED TO SUCCEED HIM.

DECEMBER 3, 2006: U.S. MILITARY DEATHS REACH 3,000.

JANUARY 10, 2007: PRESIDENT BUSH COMMITS ALMOST 30,000 MORE AMERICAN TROOPS TO IRAQ, IN WHAT BECOMES KNOWN AS THE SURGE.

JULY 12, 2007: THE WHITE HOUSE SAYS THAT IRAQ HAS MADE SATISFACTORY PROGRESS ON 8 OF 18 POLITICAL AND SECURITY BENCHMARKS OF THEIR SUCCESS. EIGHT ARE CALLED UNSATISFACTORY AND TWO ARE SAID TO BE TOO EARLY TO TELL. OTHERS CLAIM A LESSER SUCCESS.

ON SEPTEMBER 14, DEFENSE SECRETARY GATES SAID THAT HE HOPED TO CUT U.S. FORCES IN IRAQ TO 100,000 TROOPS FROM ITS CURRENT 169,000 BY THE END OF 2008. BUT SUPPORTING THE PETRAEUS POLICY, HE WENT ON...

AT THE SAME TIME, A BILL WAS PROPOSED BY VIRGINIA DEMOCRATIC SENATOR JIM WEBB TO REQUIRE TROOPS TO SPEND AS MUCH TIME AT HOME AS ON THEIR MOST RECENT TOUR OVERSEAS, WHICH ULTIMATELY WOULD FORCE AN EARLIER RETURN OF OUR TROOPS FROM IRAQ.

THE CONSEQUENCES OF FAILURE IN IRAQ...

...WOULD BE DISASTROUS. NOT JUST FOR IRAQ, BUT FOR THE REGION, FOR THE U.S. AND FOR THE WORLD.

BUT LIKE SEVEN SIMILAR PREVIOUS DEMOCRATIC MEASURES TO CURTAIL THE WAR, THIS TOO COULD NOT GAIN ENOUGH REPUBLICAN SUPPORT TO PASS.

ON SEPTEMBER 17, ANGRY IRAQI AUTHORITIES CANCELED THE LICENSE OF THE AMERICAN SECURITY FIRM BLACKWATER USA, WHOSE GUARDS WERE ACCUSED OF KILLING AT LEAST EIGHT IRAQI CIVILIANS WHILE PROTECTING A STATE DEPARTMENT MOTORCADE ON SEPTEMBER 16.

THIS BROUGHT TO LIGHT THE ENORMOUS USE IN IRAQ OF PRIVATE CONTRACTORS, WHO ARE NOT BOUND BY MILITARY OR CIVILIAN LAW. THE NUMBER OF THEIR PERSONNEL HAS BEEN REPORTED TO BE BETWEEN 126,000 AND 180,000, WITH AS MANY AS 48,000 OF THEM BEING SECURITY GUARDS.

THE NUMBER OF SECURITY GUARDS IS SIX TIMES THE AMOUNT OF PRESENT BRITISH TROOPS.

...THEY HAVE LONG BEEN ACCUSED OF SPEEDING THROUGH BAGHDAD STREETS AND SHOOTING INDISCRIMINATELY AT ANYONE DEEMED A THREAT. IT HAS BEEN REPORTED THAT 916 CONTRACTORS THUS FAR HAVE BEEN KILLED AND 12,000 WOUNDED IN THE IRAQ WAR.

ON SEPTEMBER 19, PRIME MINISTER MALIKI CLAIMED THERE HAD BEEN SIX PREVIOUS CASES IN WHICH BLACKWATER GUARDS HAD KILLED IRAQIS, "CREATING A STATE OF TENSION AND ANGER AMONG US ALL." HOWEVER, ON SEPTEMBER 21, BLACKWATER USA RESUMED ESCORTING CONVOYS OF AMERICAN DIPLOMATS. NO EXPLANATION WAS GIVEN.

EPILOGUE

THIS IS AN INCOMPLETE STORY OF AN INCOMPLETE WAR.

THE FOLLOWING WAS REPORTED EVEN AS WE WENT TO PRESS:

SEPTEMBER 7, 2007

THE *LOS ANGELES TIMES* REPORTS THAT THE COST OF THE WARS IN IRAQ AND AFGHANISTAN HAS BALLOONED FROM $33.8 BILLION IN 2001-2002 TO $94 BILLION IN 2004, TO $122 BILLION IN 2006, TO MORE THAN $170 BILLION IN 2007, TO AN ESTIMATED $195 BILLION IN 2008, AND, EVEN WITH A POSSIBLE REDUCTION IN THE SIZE OF OUR MILITARY FORCES, TO BETWEEN $170 BILLION TO $200 BILLION IN 2009. AT THE START OF THE IRAQ WAR, THE BUSH ADMINISTRATION CLAIMED THAT THE COST OF OUSTING SADDAM HUSSEIN AND INSTALLING A NEW GOVERNMENT IN IRAQ WOULD COST A TOTAL OF BETWEEN $50 BILLION AND $60 BILLION.

MARCH 13, 2008

GEN. DAVID H. PETRAEUS DECLARES THAT IRAQI LEADERS HAVE THUS FAR FAILED TO TAKE ADVANTAGE OF THE REDUCTION OF VIOLENCE IN THEIR COUNTRY TO RESOLVE THEIR POLITICAL PROBLEMS. "NO ONE THERE," HE SAID, "HAD SEEN SUFFICIENT PROGRESS BY ANY MEANS IN THE AREA OF NATIONAL RECONCILIATION."

MARCH 24, 2008

THE *LOS ANGELES TIMES* REPORTS A SIZABLE DROP IN THE MONTHLY TOLL OF U.S. DEATHS IN IRAQ. IN MAY 2007, THERE WERE MORE THAN 125 DEATHS, AND AMERICAN DEATHS WERE REDUCED TO LESS THAN 30 BY MARCH 2008. HOWEVER, IN APRIL 2008, THAT SAME NEWSPAPER REPORTS THAT THE FIGURE JUMPED TO 50, THE HIGHEST LOSS OF U.S. LIVES SINCE SEPTEMBER 2007, WHEN THERE HAD BEEN 65.

APRIL 8, 2008

GENERAL PETRAEUS APPEARS BEFORE THE SENATE ARMED SERVICES COMMITTEE, WHERE HE STATES THAT "SINCE SEPTEMBER, LEVELS OF VIOLENCE AND CIVILIAN DEATHS HAVE BEEN REDUCED SUBSTANTIALLY," THAT AL QAEDA HAS BEEN DEALT "SERIOUS BLOWS, AND IRAQI SECURITY FORCES HAVE GROWN IN THEIR CAPABILITIES. NONETHELESS," HE CONTINUES, "THE SITUATION IN CERTAIN AREAS IS STILL UNSATISFACTORY, AND INNUMERABLE CHALLENGES REMAIN." HE ADDS, "THE PROGRESS MADE SINCE LAST SPRING IS FRAGILE AND REVERSIBLE."

JUNE 6, 2008

THE *NEW YORK TIMES* REPORTS THAT, AFTER A FIVE-YEAR INVESTIGATION, THE SENATE SELECT COMMITTEE ON INTELLIGENCE CONCLUDED THAT PRESIDENT BUSH, VICE PRESIDENT CHENEY, AND OTHER HIGH-RANKING OFFICIALS SYSTEMATICALLY SELECTED AND EXAGGERATED INTELLIGENCE TO MAKE THE CASE FOR INVADING IRAQ.

SO FAR, THIS HAS BEEN THE COSTLIEST OF ALL OUR WARS, THE LONGEST OF ALL OUR WARS, ONE OF THE LEAST POPULAR OF ALL OUR WARS, AND, PERHAPS, THE SINGLE MOST DAMAGING WAR TO THE REPUTATION OF THIS NATION.

IT IS IMPORTANT, THE AUTHORS BELIEVE, THAT WE TELL THIS STORY AS PLAINLY AS POSSIBLE. IT IS TOO IMPORTANT THAT WE ALL UNDERSTAND EXACTLY WHAT HAS TAKEN PLACE THESE LAST SIX YEARS. WE HOPE THAT WE HAVE SUCCEEDED.

WE'D LIKE TO END THIS WITH AN OBSERVATION DAVID H. PETRAEUS MADE IN HIS DOCTORAL DISSERTATION AT PRINCETON IN 1987. TITLED "THE AMERICAN MILITARY AND THE LESSONS OF VIETNAM," AND REFERRING TO THE FAILURES OF THE SOVIET UNION IN AFGHANISTAN, THE GENERAL WROTE... "AFTER ALL, IF A COUNTRY WITH RELATIVELY FEW PUBLIC OPINION CONCERNS OR MORAL COMPUNCTIONS ABOUT ITS TACTICS CANNOT BEAT A BUNCH OF ILL-EQUIPPED AFGHAN TRIBESMEN, WHAT DOES THAT SAY ABOUT THE ABILITY OF THE UNITED STATES--WITH ITS DOMESTIC CONSTRAINTS, STATUTORY LIMITATIONS, MORAL INHIBITIONS, AND ZEALOUS INVESTIGATORY REPORTERS--TO CARRY OUT A SUCCESSFUL ACTION AGAINST A GUERRILLA FORCE?"